STEPHEN KING

IT

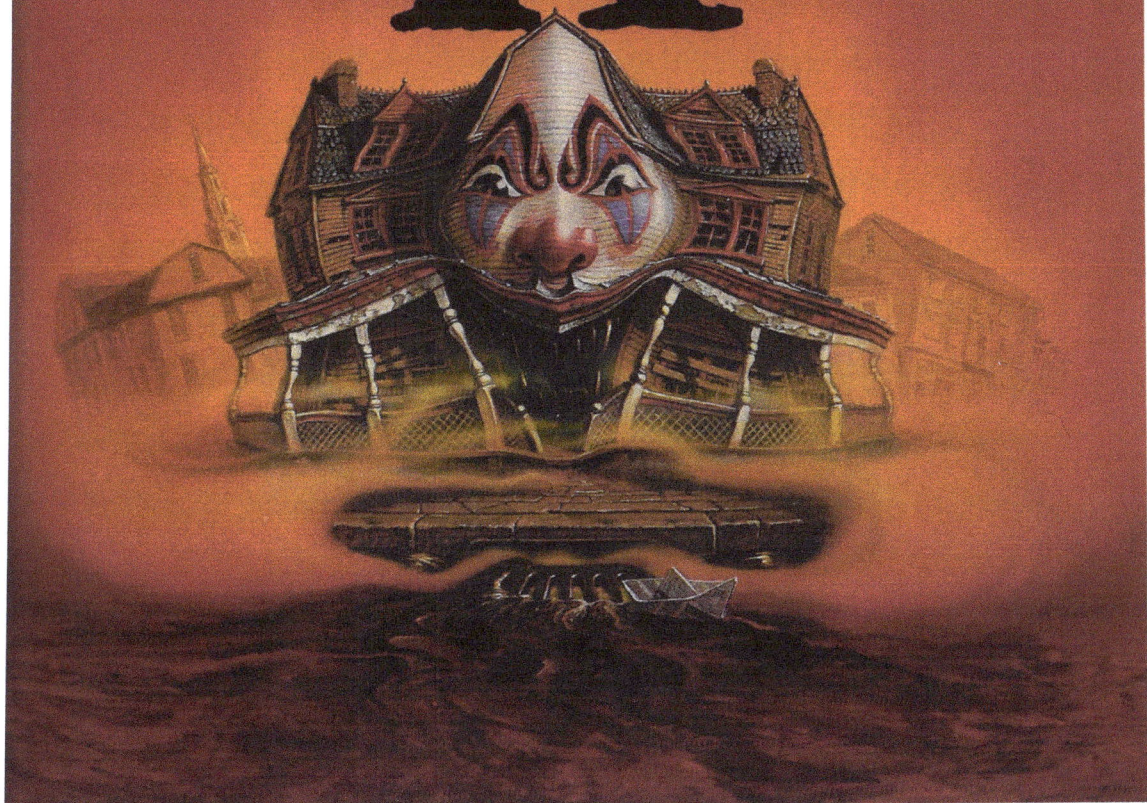

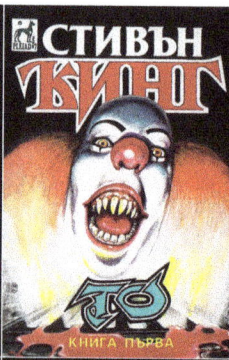
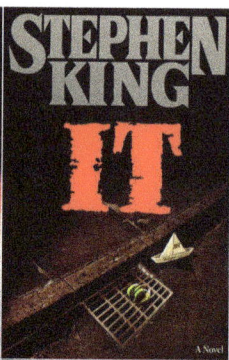
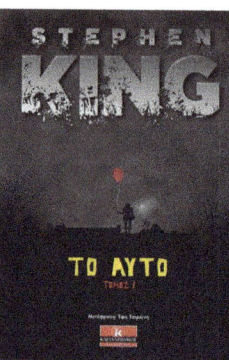

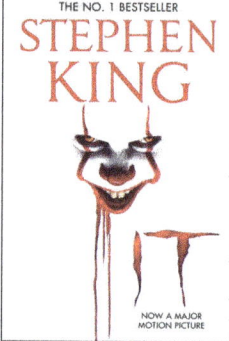
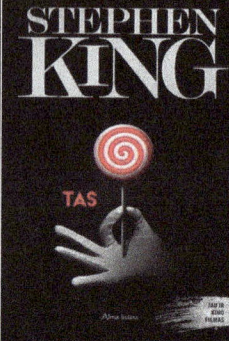
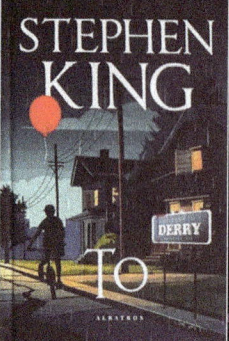
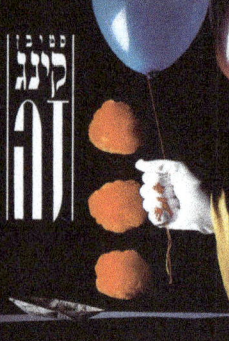

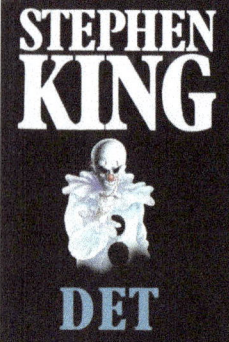
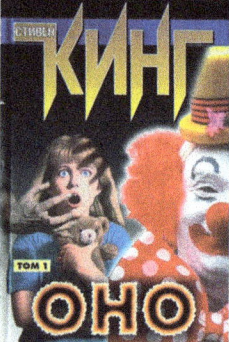
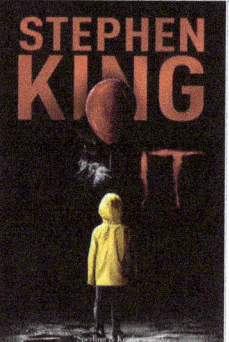

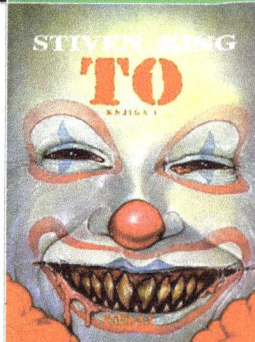
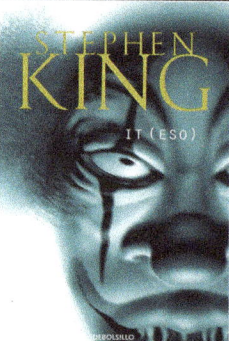
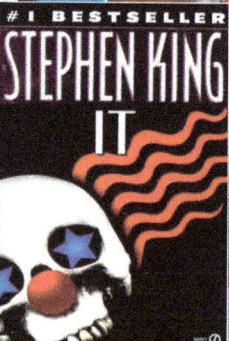
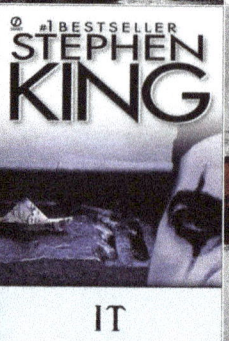
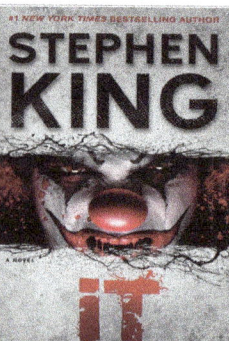
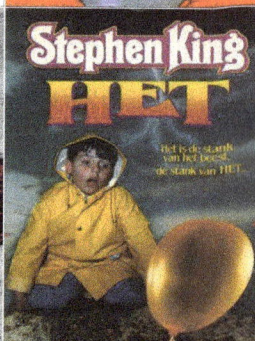
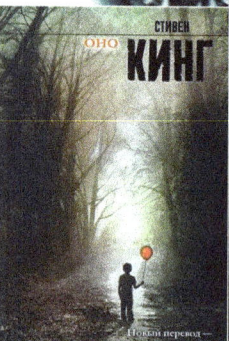

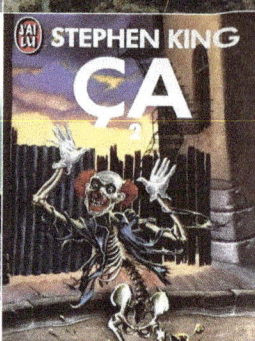

STEPHEN KING

CALENDAR
-2026-

PENNYWISE HAS ARRIVED!

IT

40th Anniversary

Written and Edited by Dave Hinchberger

Also features Artwork by Glenn Chadbourne

Graphic Design/Layout by Bryan McAllister

OVERLOOK CONNECTION PRESS

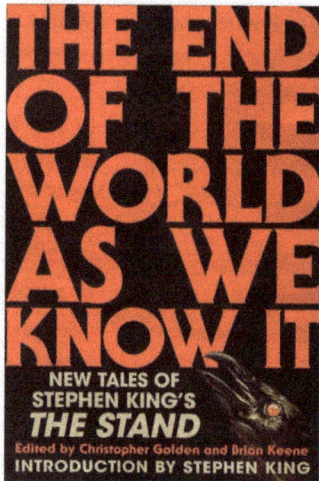

PENNYWISE TURNS FORTY!

by Dave Hinchberger

Can you fathom that it's been forty years since *IT*, Pennywise, was unleashed on the world of horror fiction? If you're like me, back in 1986 when Stephen Kings immense tome, *IT*, was released I was absolutely elated. The buildup had been coming for some time about this new monster King created for us, IT! A new King novel was always celebrated, but it was also because here, in my hands, I held an incredibly (what I assumed would be a *huge* story) large printed volume, that weighs 3.96 pounds (yes, I weighed the Viking hardcover!). Little did I know that the weight of the book exemplified the weight of the story.

Yes, I was stoked, it was like receiving three novels in one with all the twists and turns within the 1138 pages. I was going to take time with this one. As we discovered, Stephen King threw everything into the horror kitchen sink that is *IT*. He's mentioned this in many interviews how he purposely included the horrors of his childhood, from fiction, film, and television. It was fun to see what It would bare, fangs to claws, and every nightmare in between, page after page.

Naturally *IT* was picked up for film rights, which eventually became the 1990 ABC miniseries starring Tim Curry. Eventually it got the film treatment it deserved with Pennywise helmed by Bill Skarsgård, with his creepy lip curling move. This time fleshing out more from the novel, from Andy (director) and Barbra (producer) Muschietti, delivering an impressive 1.2 billion in ticket sales making it the No. 1 horror franchise of all time. It's no wonder

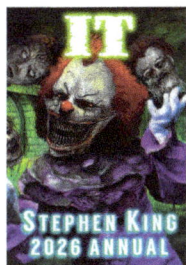

Halloween is the no. 1 holiday now with sales like that. As we go to print *Welcome To Derry* is going to begin airing on HBO October 26th a new series taking *IT* even farther, rather, backwards to 1962, in this prequel.

This year we have seen seven separate Stephen King releases, albeit one being an anthology, *The End of the World as We Know It: New Tales of The Stand* (Stephen King wrote the introduction). A new novel, *Never Flinch*, and the mini hardcover of *The Life of Chuck* (with a page flip movie in the book). The first trade hardcover of *The Long Walk* celebrating the film release. Then King's unique take on *Hansel and Gretal*. Up next, *The Running Man* with its first-ever hardcover. To top it all off, the anniversary edition of *Firestarter* arrived in October. Granted, several are reprints in new formats, but they are all becoming part of Stephen King libraries all over the world.

Have fun visiting with forty years of Pennywise, *IT* himself, in this year's King Calendar. If you enjoy the King Calendar you would also enjoy the *2026 Stephen King Annual: IT* it's twice the size and features so much more on Stephen King's *IT* Fortieth Anniversary.

Be prepared for the chills and squeals for the *2027 The Shining Calendar* and *2027 Annual* coming fall of 2026.

Now, IT's time to put on your deadlights.. and float… kiddies.

– Dave Hinchberger

Pennywise in the Flesh:
An Excerpt of my exclusive 1990 interview with Tim Curry on the set of Stephen King's *IT*

by Steve Newton

"I Think of Him... as a Smile Gone Bad..." – Tim Curry

Steve Newton recently unearthed his original interview with Tim Curry on the set of the 1990 ABC miniseries event of *IT*. Originally published in an edited version in *Fangoria* (#99) magazine in December of 1990, here is an excerpt from his unexpurgated interview (full interview available in *The 2026 Stephen King Annual*). As he points out here his was the only interview allowed with Tim Curry on the set during filming. Thanks for sharing to a new audience, Steve!

– Dave Hinchberger, editor.

IT was a beautiful summer day–June 27, 1990–when I ventured out to Vancouver's sprawling Stanley Park to interview Tim Curry.

At the time the legendary British actor was filming a two-part TV "miniseries" based on Stephen King's widely acclaimed 1986 horror novel, *IT*.

I was on assignment for New York-based *Fangoria* magazine, and apparently it was the only publication given access to Curry, because no other journalist in the entire world got to meet him on the set and get the scoop.

Just me. Yep, I'm bragging a bit.

Anyway, Curry was starring as an ancient cosmic evil that took the form of a child-killing clown called Pennywise. I got to sit down with him while he ate some lunch in full evil-clown mode, with makeup-FX artist Bart Mixon standing by to add comments here and there and dab at Curry's face now and then.

Steve Newton: First off, I was wondering if you could give me the rundown on what your character is in *IT*. Obviously a clown. Pennywhistle? I haven't finished the book yet...

Tim Curry: Pennywise.

SN: ...it's a long book.

TC: Pennywise.

SN: Pennywise, yeah.

TC: Well. He's the villain of the piece. The city or the town of Derry, in Maine, has been terrorized every 30 years by something that these kids have come to call It. And It mostly takes the form of a clown called Pennywise, which they first encounter...well they first understand who he is when they find an old, I guess, a Victorian, is it a Victorian postcard? (Makeup FX artist Bart Mixon: "1930"). 1930 postcard, of the circus coming to town or whatever. Is it earlier than that? Isn't it 1890 or

something? (Mixon: "Yeah, and then they see a photo from 1929."). Yeah. And then they see a photo from the '20s or the '30s, which comes to life, in a sort of a circus parade. Comes right up to the surface of this postcard and tries to get out.

Basically, I guess he's just pure evil, really, and he can also metamorphose into various other forms—mostly into the image that whoever he's appearing to fears most. Or he can also sort of seductively become other people. At one point he turns into somebody's dead father, at another point he turns into the girl that the guy's in love with. And he uh.. we won't tell you what he turns into at the end. He'll probably tell you [referring to Mixon]. But basically, he's completely irredeemable; he's the kind of chap that's entirely without charm.

And what's fun about him is that a clown is traditionally a very cozy, comforting kind of cheery image, and Pennywise is none of these things. I think of him all the time as a smile gone bad—that's my image for him.

SN: Is this your first time in makeup since *Rocky Horror*?

TC: Um, what, in prosthetic makeup you mean? I didn't have prosthetic makeup in that. Well, no, I did Legend. Which was extremely prosthetic. Well and I also, in England I did a series on the life of William Shakespeare and I played him from like 19 to his middle-50s. I lost a great deal of my hair, they shaved my hair back gradually because he lost his. And then I had a great deal of latex old-age makeup done which was sort of nothing compared to this kind of stuff.

The screen's most famous transvestite adopts a deceptively cheery face to play the child-stalking villain of "It."

King's Lot

Clowning Around With Tim Curry

By STEVE NEWTON

Local Transvestite Makes Good: *Rocky Horror* just celebrated its 15th anniversary, and (at presstime) is set to hit video this fall.

Leave it to Pennywise to ruin a solemn reunion portrait.

28 · FANGORIA #99

SN: Do you mind being in that much makeup? Are you used to it after *Legend*?

TC: I don't think anybody likes it really. I mean it's fun to evolve it. It's great fun when you're actually working it, making it part of yourself, and finding out what it can do. And one of the nice things about a very broad, feature-changing makeup is that you have no personal history with it, you know. I mean I don't think there's an actual actor or an actress in the world who actually likes his or her face, so to get rid of all that stuff in front of a camera is totally useful. Because if you're looking like this you don't have to worry about angles too much, you know. It's not about looking good (laughs). It's about being effective.

SN: How long does it take to get that on, from start to finish?

TC: They've got it down to about three hours now. (Mixon: "It took longer at first just 'cause we were figuring out the brows and the mouth,"). It always does. In the beginning it always takes a long time.

SN: Are you a horror or fantasy genre fan yourself? Obviously you got sort of pegged in *Rocky Horror*. And then you went on to *Legend*.

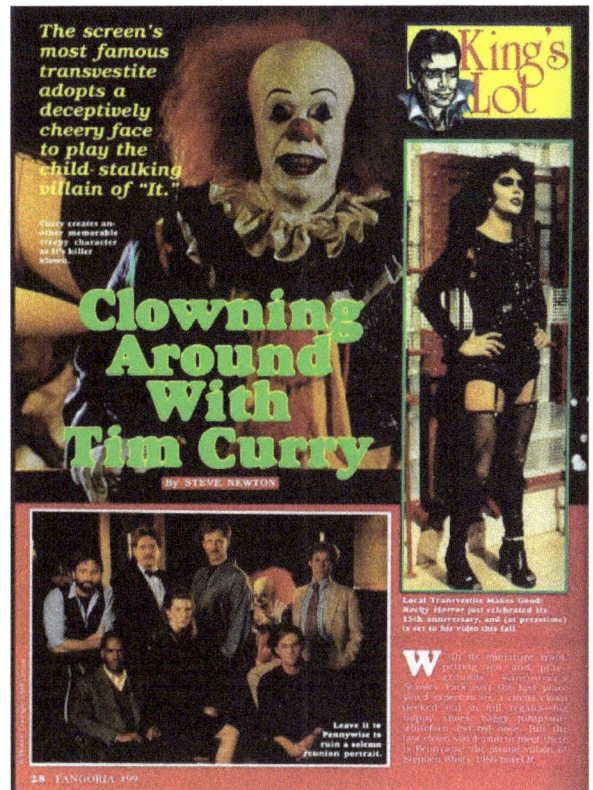

Curry's face may be hidden behind makeup, but that devilish charm still shines through.

Frank N. Furter gets a little smack treatment in his hot pink lab.

Although there already exists one *Rocky Horror* "sequel"—1981's Curry-less *Shock Treatment*—the actor says that the title *Rocky Horror Picture Show: 2* has been registered, and that a direct follow-up to the original is in the planning stages.

"There's not an actor in the world who likes their face, so to get rid of all that [on camera] is terribly useful."

TC: I'm not particularly, actually. Richard O'Brien, who wrote *Rocky*, very much was, and is, but it's his obsession, not mine. I mean, I'm fascinated by movie villains—I enjoyed Lon Chaney. But in some ways I think that horror movies have got a little too far away from the mind. I mean we had a much more prosthetic version of this makeup–which was very scary looking, and beautifully executed–but did too much work by itself. And I personally think that what is the most horrifying is the moment of decision behind somebody's eyes when they decide to kill somebody, rather than a pint of blood and a pound-and-a-half of latex.

Which is not to say that all of this isn't useful. I just think that it's…I think myself to a certain degree that it's kind of taken over, and that one sacrifices the human element at great risk. But this is obviously an actor's viewpoint. (Mixon: "We'll talk later.") Well, you know, there was a classic day in the trailer when I said "I'm not here to get you an Emmy."

SN: Are you a Stephen King fan?

TC: Well, I always get the books. Yeah. I mean, yes. I mean, he's an extremely entertaining writer; I think he's really good at that stuff.

SN: Yeah. I liked *The Dead Zone*. That was probably my favorite that he's done so far.

TC: I liked *The Shining* a lot too. I would have liked to have done *The Shining*. I mean he certainly gives a lot of acting opportunities.

SN: Yeah. I heard they're gonna make *Graveyard Shift*, from one of his *Night Shift* stories. And, of course, *The Stand*'s been in the works for ages, with Romero I think.

TC: (Mixon: "Romero's owned it for like ten years.") Has he? Is he the guy who did *The Night of the Living Dead*? (Mixon: "Right. *Creepshow*. It's just it's so big. And now it's even bigger.") I just started that. I'm gonna be on that for months. Except I read pretty fast.

SN: Thanks very much for the interview.

TC: You bet.

You can read the complete unexpurgated interview with Tim Curry, by Steve Newton, in the *2026 Stephen King Annual*. Available at **StephenKingCatalog.com** and **Amazon.com**

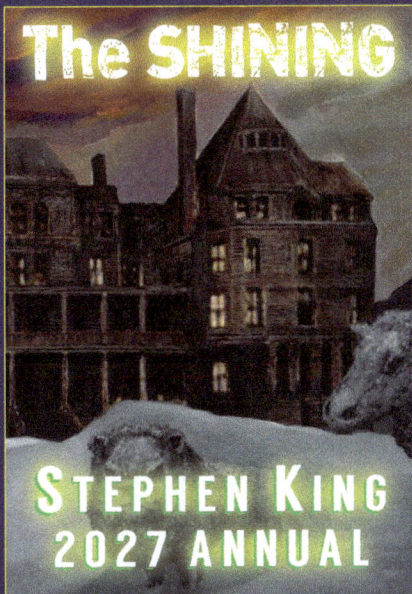

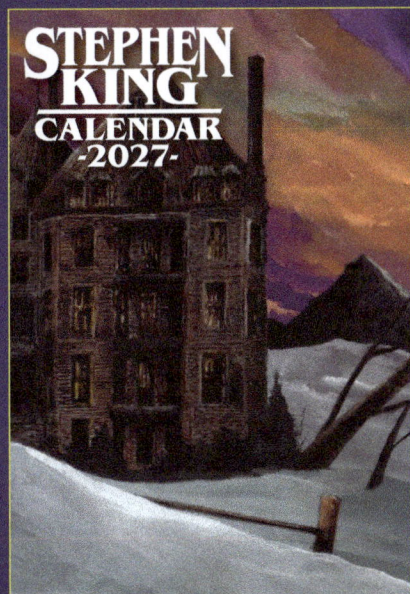

STEPHEN KING'S *IT* – The Miniseries (1990)

by L.L. Soares

[THE SCENE: OUTSIDE at night. First, the camera pans over a neon sign that reads "CHOP SUEY" in red letters and "CHINESE KITCHEN" in blue. We then go INSIDE, where a crane shot shows us an elaborately ornate interior and leads us to our HOST, who is sitting at a table near the back of the restaurant, snacking on Crab Rangoons.]

HOST: Welcome, I'm your host, L.L. Soares, happy to hold the lantern as we take a walk down memory lane with a bit of Stephen King nostalgia. Today, we're going to talk about the first adaptation of his novel *IT*, which aired in two parts on ABC television in 1990. *IT* would make ABC a go-to network for King adaptations, paving the way for *The Tommyknockers* (1993), *The Stand* (1994), and *The Langoliers* (1995). *IT* originally aired during November "sweeps month," when networks pulled out their big guns for ratings. And it was a hit, bringing in 30 million viewers for the two-night event (it originally aired on November 18th and 20th of 1990).

IT was the second time TV had adapted a King novel as a "miniseries." The first was Tobe Hooper's memorable version of *Salem's Lot* in 1979.

I remember watching *IT* at the time, excited about the prospect of seeing King's epic on the (small) screen. This excitement would only be magnified when ABC took a stab at adapting *The Stand* four years later.

Needless to say, because of the restrictions of network television, there were lots of limitations, and a lot of the story was left out of the screenplay (written by Lawrence D. Cohen, who also adapted the Brian De Palma film version of *Carrie*, 1976). The story would be much-improved later in the superior film adaptations directed by Andy Muschietti in 2017 and 2019, but back in 1990, this was all we had, folks.

One of the big draws of the television version, aside from it being treated as "prestige television" by the network, was the casting, which included several big television stars of the time. Richard Thomas ("John Boy" Walton himself from *The Waltons*, a major show that had nine seasons) played Bill Denbrough, who, as an adult, has become a writer of horror fiction. John Ritter (Jack Tripper on the popular comedy *Three's Company*) was Ben Hanscom, now a famous architect. Harry Anderson (Judge Stone from the original version of *Night Court*), played Richie Tozier, the joker of the group, now a professional comedian. Tim Reid (DJ Venus Flytrap from the radio station sitcom *WKRP In Cincinnati*) was Mike Hanlon, who has never

Annette O'Toole, John Ritter, Tim Reid, Harry Anderson (l-r) and Dennis Christopher (seated, front) star as childhood friends reunited to confront an evil entity (Tim Curry, lurking), in the ABC miniseries, "STEPHEN KING'S IT," airing during the 1990-91 season on the ABC Television Network.   Photo credit: Bob D'Amico/ABC.

IT cast press photo, ABC 1990

STEPHEN KING'S
IT

ANNETTE O'TOOLE stars as
Beverly Marsh.

IT press photo, Lorimar Television 1990

left their hometown of Derry, Maine, and who has become the town's librarian (and tireless sentry against the return of evil).

Also cast were familiar faces (at the time) Annette O'Toole as Beverly Marsh, who grew up with an abusive, alcoholic father and who is in another abusive relationship when we meet her as an adult; Richard Masur as Stanley Uris, the literal Boy Scout of the group as kids, who is now a real estate agent; and Dennis Christopher (also in the much-praised bicycle-themed movie *Breaking Away*, 1979, and the horror flick *Fade To Black*, 1980) as Eddie Kaspbrak, who was the sickly asthmatic kid in the past, and is now the owner of a successful limo service, though still sickly (although his health is directly tied to his mother, even as an adult). Also on board is British actress Olivia Hussy (from Franco Zeffirelli's *Romeo and Juliet*, 1968, and Bob Clark's *Black Christmas*) in a mostly thankless role as Bill's wife, Audra. And that's Michael Cole himself from the *Mod Squad* as the adult Henry Bowers, freed from the psych ward to do Pennywise's bidding.

But perhaps the most thrilling casting choice was Tim Curry – Dr. Frank-N-Furter himself in the cult classic *The Rocky Horror Picture Show* – as Pennywise the Dancing Clown, who, as we all know, is the villain of this piece. Made to

look friendly (except for when those monster teeth appear!) so that he could lure his child victims in, and talking and acting like an old-time Borscht Belt comedian, Curry was perfect in the role (although it can be argued that Bill Sarsgaard's later version upped the creepiness factor a lot) and was the first choice of director Tommy Lee Wallace.

While the adult stars are the reason that some people tuned in to the miniseries, I have to admit, the flashbacks to when they were kids are much more powerful. You would think that kids would be more scared and reluctant to take on a child-eating demon, but the thing is, they're a scrappy bunch and even though they're learning as they go along how to deal with Pennywise, they're smart and they learn quickly. It's the 12-year-old gang who are the real stars here, including Jonathan Brandis as the young Bill Denbrough – who takes turns being the "heart" of the group with Beverly Marsh (Emily Perkins); Brandon Crane as overweight but clever Ben Hanscom; Adam Faraizl as asthmatic Eddie Kaspbrak; genre mainstay Seth Green as the young joker of the group, Richie Tozier; Ben Heller as Stanley Uris, who seems to always be in his Boy Scout uniform; and Marlon Taylor as the young Mike Hanlon, the newest kid in town.

Part 1 introduces us to the players, as both adults and children, but the kids just seem more relatable and heroic as it all unfolds. They are sort of ready for Pennywise, because they've been training for it with their interactions with the main local bully, Henry Bowers (played by Jarred Blancard at age 14, slightly older than the "Losers' Club" members) and his gang of Fonzi-lookalike weasels (although the show *Happy Days* ended in 1984, it had certainly left its mark on popular culture). A lot of the kid bullies in King's work seem borderline psychotic, and Henry is no exception. He pulls a switchblade on Ben, coming very close to cutting him with it, and threatens to put a cherry bomb in Mike Hanlon's pocket. You wonder, if unrestrained by his friends' reactions, just how far Henry would go? Is he capable of murder, even as a teenager? It certainly seems so. We know his father beats him, so he has trauma of his own,

Art by Allen Koszowski

and he's more than happy to inflict his own pain on others. He's like a rehearsal stand-in for the evil clown, and the scene where the outcast kids throw rocks at their bullies prepares us for the final showdown with Pennywise in the bowels of the town's sewer system.

In contrast, the adult versions of the characters seem more one-dimensional. We get glimpses of their hopes and dreams, their motivations, and miseries, but there's no time here to flesh them out completely (like in a 1,168-page novel) and a lot of the shorthand used to familiarize ourselves with them borders on stereotypes (okay, in some instances, almost total stereotypes!). Bill is the soulful one. Richie the comic relief. Ben is the overweight kid who wants to be loved. Eddie, the sickly kid who is capable of heroism when pushed to the edge, etc.

While we can say that the adults are less fleshed out because of the time constraints, the interesting thing is that the child versions of these characters, who dominate the first part of the two-part miniseries, are able to transcend their limitations a lot more effectively. They have arguably as much screen time as the adult versions, and yet they're more thoughtful, resilient, and creative, and their plight seems to pack more of an emotional punch. The adults, who are older and bigger and who have

already faced Pennywise once before, should be smarter, but seem to be at a disadvantage in comparison – with one member (Stanley) even committing suicide rather than going back to Derry for another battle with Pennywise. The adults are more susceptible to fear, which is just the way Pennywise wants them.

The 1990 miniseries is inferior in just about every way to the Andy Muschietti retelling(s) of the tale. With bigger budgets, more time to expand on the themes, and just overall better quality, the 2017 and 2019 flicks are terrific, and while I am sure there are debates about which version of Pennywise is better – Tim Curry's more jokey clown or Bill Skarsgard more "alien" version who seems less human and more unpredictable – I find them both kind of cool. Curry was the defining version of Pennywise for decades, and if we remembered nothing else from the TV miniseries, we remembered him. To make the new version look and act the same would feel like a cheat, like a Xerox (remember those?). Muschietti's choice to make his clown more "other" actually adds to the creepiness of the proceedings, and makes the character

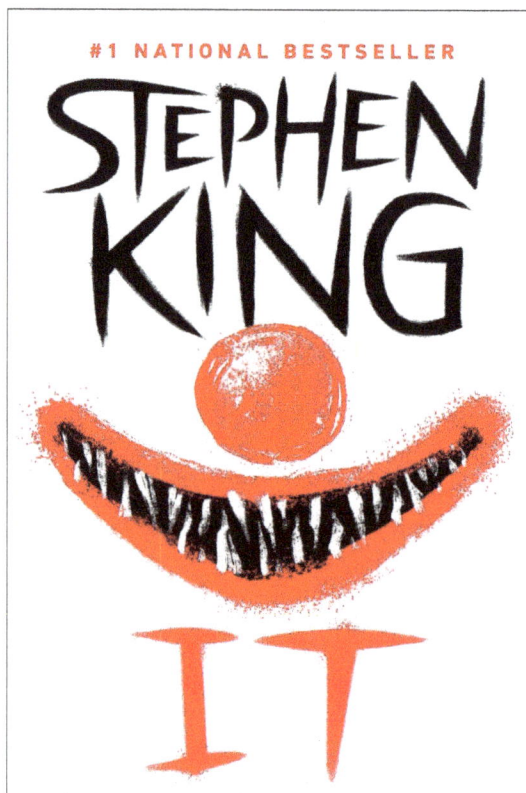

IT 2017 Scribner trade paperback

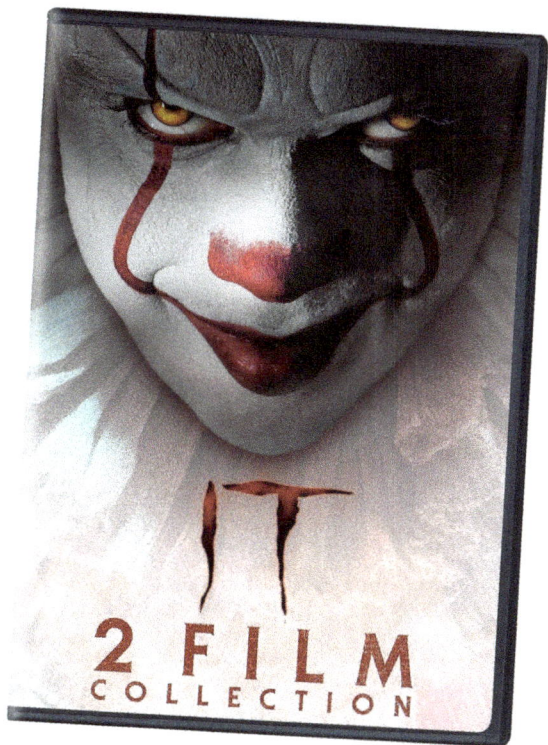

Warner Home Video 2019

that stay with us, whether we want them to or not.

Watching the miniseries again after all these years (it has been edited into one movie now, sadly, and is available for streaming on HBO MAX) brought back mixed feelings for me. How it could have been so much better – but also, how I was able to enjoy the charms that it still has. And, despite its flaws, it was a very pleasant look backwards.

[THE HOST looks across the table at the empty chair, just in time to see a red balloon pop up from beneath the table and float up above his head.]

Well, it looks like my dinner guest is arriving. I wonder what mood he'll be in. Quick with a joke or quick with a kill? Wish me luck, dear friends. Let's just hope this won't be the last you see of me!

-(Camera slowly FADES TO BLACK)-

all Skarsgard's (I'd go as far as to say I like Skarsgard better, but I'd prefer to say I like them both, since I'm a Curry fan, too, and they're so different).

A perfect example is a scene that has become iconic. Little Georgie Denbrough (Tony Dakota in the miniseries) is floating a paper boat his older brother has made for him, when he encounters a certain clown in the sewer drain. The version in the miniseries is memorable, the version in Muschietti's film is even bigger and better, but both stay with you long after the credits roll.

Despite its shortcomings, I remember really enjoying the 1990 version of *IT* when it first aired, and it went a long way to making later King miniseries seem like special events. There is a reason why King is the genre powerhouse he's become (and has been for so long now). He's just a master storyteller. And even inferior adaptations of his work can have aspects that are worth remembering – or, rather,

Welcome to My Town, Derry.

by Chris Jiggins

1962 - The scene opens with a barber shaving his customer in front of a window looking out onto downtown Derry, Maine. I walk into frame, out of focus in the background, then stop mid-step. The barber notices, shifting the camera's focus to me. He steps outside, razor in hand, to investigate my sudden apprehension. The camera follows him through the door and onto the street, revealing Derry citizens from all walks of life suddenly troubled by yet another threat to their dreary small town. Cut!

A week earlier, in April 2024, I was fitted and costumed to play the part of a 1960s bookstore owner in HBO's *Welcome to Derry*. Approximately ten years prior, New Line Cinema announced that it was developing an adaptation of Stephen King's *IT*. Within two years of the announcement, crews arrived in my idyllic hometown of Port Hope, Ontario, Canada, renowned for its historical architecture and quaint shops and restaurants, to begin filming *IT*. The decision to choose Port Hope as Derry, due to its beauty that contrasts with the darkness within the story, transformed a quiet small town into a mecca for horror fans from around the world.

Like many kids my age, I discovered Pennywise through the 1990 miniseries. Burnt into my memory is the image of the double-VHS cover sitting front and centre in the horror section at my local Showtime Video. Growing up in Port Hope in the late 1980s and 1990s in a town with a population of 12,500, I related to the Losers' Club. I spent my summer days meeting up with friends and riding our bikes all over town, exploring paths along the Ganaraska River and through the trails of our very own Barrens. We spent aimless days throwing rocks at trees and hiding from the bigger kids in our hideout in the woods. So, in late 2015, when it was announced, with seemingly minimal fanfare around town, that

Chris Jiggins, bookstore owner in *Welcome to Derry*

Port Hope was selected to portray Derry in a new adaptation of *IT*, I was excited to revisit the novel for the first time in decades—this time with my hometown in mind. Small-town life in Stephen King's Maine mirrored the small-town life of my Ontario, minus the cosmic horror, of course.

I was immersed in the book when crews began arriving to transform Port Hope into Derry for the first time in July 2016. In a matter of days, American flags replaced Canadian flags, 2010's Port Hope storefronts became 1980's Derry storefronts, the town hall turned into the Derry Public Library, the Capitol Theatre marquee promoted late 80's horror films, and a giant plastic Paul Bunyan graced Memorial Park. The filming that took place in the sweltering summer of 2016 was big news for my small town.

The residential streets I biked on as a kid became those of the Losers' Club.

IT did for Port Hope what *Jaws* did for Martha's Vineyard, and the town solidified its reputation as a must-visit destination for horror movie enthusiasts.

I conceived the idea for an Instagram account to not only celebrate the filming locations of the highest-grossing horror film of all time, while sharing pictures of my hometown with fellow King fans, but to serve as a tourism account for Derry, Maine, mimicking the hundreds of existing Maine social media tourism accounts. *Discover Derry, Maine*, a name borrowed from the novel and visible on background posters in the film, gained popularity as the buzz for the sequel grew in the late spring and early summer of 2018.

In late spring, shortly after WB announced the adult cast for the sequel, production held an extras casting call for locals in an empty Canadian Tire store—the future site of the production's base camp—for a film called *Largo*. The title didn't fool anyone. Thousands of people showed up—the line lasting nearly four hours—to fill out paperwork and get their headshot taken in the hopes that they would get to be an apathetic Derry citizen; I was one of them.

I continued to play the part of a social media location scout, photographing and posting potential Derry locations, when the *Bangor Daily News* contacted me. The Stephen King beat writer pitched using various images of mine to compare Port Hope to Derry's original inspiration, Bangor, Maine. I sent a few quotes and high-quality photos, and the article was published on July 11, the same day filming on *IT: Chapter Two* officially began in Toronto.

I managed to peek around to see the six surviving adult losers walking together toward me down the main street. I managed to cross the bridge once the shot ended to confirm that it was the stars of the film, not stand-ins, who were hanging around my hometown.

I popped into a tiny coffee shop on the corner where a lineup of five ends at the door, I was shocked to see the three of the "Losers'" laughing at the counter: there was Mike,

Capitol Theater, Derry, Maine (Port Hope, Ontario)

Richie, and Eddie enjoying a morning out in an alternate Derry free from the taunts of and terrors of Pennywise.

Walking around town felt like being on the Warner Bros. backlot. A massive crane stretched above the street outside the Capitol Theatre with a giant diffuser hanging from a wire to light the scene below. Seasoned crew members dragged large cables along the curb as Bill Hader passed by with a nod. Nicholas Hamilton exited a café, passing James McAvoy signing autographs and crew members lining up child-sized bikes along the wall. Further up the street, the second unit filmed Isiah Mustafah wandering the streets, while the child actors began showing up outside the theatre. A month later, Paul Bunyan returned to town, this time bigger and bulkier for the sequel.

I returned to the park the next morning in time to see Pennywise emerge from a small, white makeup tent, then quickly surrounded by a crew who jockeyed him into position at the base of the statue. It's one thing to see a horror icon brought to life on the big screen, manipulated by lights and music: its bone-chilling seeing one in person, even if he's yucking it up with Bill Hader over a cup of coffee.

In September I received an email with my extras shooting schedule and details. I was to dress warmly for a week of night shoots at a 'small-town American carnival'.

Losers' Club kids, *IT*, Derry (Port Hope, Ontario)

Losers' Club adults, *IT: Chapter Two?*, Derry (Port Hope, Ontario)

Days prior, while the crew set up carnival rides in a parking lot behind the town hall, rumours circulated around town that Stephen King was coming. I didn't believe it, but sure enough, he flew into a nearby airport, then travelled roughly half an hour to Port Hope, reportedly spending five days in town hanging out on set with his grandson. During a break in filming, I caught sight of him behind Second Hand Rose and cautiously approached with a copy of my favourite book. He signed *The Stand*, 'For Chris. All the best, Stephen King - 9/11/18.' Then, after a short conversation about his time in town, I watched as Barbara Muschietti lead him away to see the nearby Paul Bunyan statue with his grandson.

My job as an extra was to roam around the fully functioning Derry Canal Days Carnival

Secondhand Rose thrift store, *Welcome to Derry* (Port Hope, Ontario)

wearing a beaver-tailed 'I Love Derry' hat and carrying a blue balloon. As a film geek, on set I spent most of my time close to the action, watching Andy direct the actors, including the legendary Canadian indie director Xavier Dolan, who portrayed Adrian Mellon.

That evening, the extras took a break for lunch back at base camp. We gathered inside an old retail space that housed the inside of the Losers' Club clubhouse, a creepy room from the Neibolt house and a rack full of costumes, including various Pennywise outfits.

IT: Chapter Two premiered to a sold-out crowd at the Capitol Theatre on September 6th, 2019.

In the fallow years between the release of *IT: Chapter Two* and the filming of *Welcome to Derry*, rumours swirled about more Derry in the spring of 2022. Every production that rolled into town in those years brought back fond memories of floating clowns and Hollywood stars, and the hope that Derry would one day return. Having kept in touch with Barbara, I, sometime in 2022, after becoming part-owner of the legendary Port Hope bookstore Furby House Books (est. 1989), reached out to the busy producer to pass along the news. Then, on a dreary February 2023 afternoon, less than a week before the official news of a prequel series broke, the door to the bookstore opened, and in walked Barbara. She came in to say hello and congratulate me on the bookstore, expressing her adoration for the shop and being back in town. Outside, her brother Andy, along with a group of presumably department heads, window-shopped while they waited for her to continue their scouting adventure. It was then, on the eve of the big announcement, that I found out that in a matter of months, Port Hope was to become Derry yet again. That afternoon, many of the crew members returned to the shop, purchasing everything from puzzles to *IT* socks. I barely held it together.

Trucks began returning to town throughout March and early April of 2023, and location crews worked to transform Port Hope into Derry. This time, it was the 1960s, and the changes nearly affected the entire downtown area (reportedly up to forty locations), including our bookstore. We became Halston Hobbies, where model planes replaced the books in the window. The fact that I was negotiating location contract terms years after I watched *IT* (2017) being made from the sidelines wasn't lost on me. I continued to document my wild journey by taking hundreds of photographs, but was strategic with what I shared, feeling, more than ever, that I was part of the *IT* family.

Filming on *Greetings from Fairview*, also known as *Welcome to Derry*, took place throughout May 2023, introducing several new locations, including the Derry Police Department, The Falcon Tavern, a built-from-scratch Derry Grill, and a downtown version of Jade of the Orient. Locations such as Second-Hand Rose and Quality Meats returned.

Running the bookstore also provided up-close access to footage shot in front of the store, including a pivotal scene featuring a new group of losers who couldn't help but notice the red balloon we had attached to our *IT* display. The store also provided me with the joy of interacting with tourists and travelling

Pennywise rides Paul Bunyon, *IT: Chapter Two*

fans from around the world, as well as meeting actors and crew.

In early March, filming took place on a country road on the outskirts of town, where the crew erected an ominous "Welcome to Derry" billboard featuring a grinning Paul Bunyan in a snowy ditch. *Greetings from Fairview* filming notices began circulating again later that month, including a notice regarding a 'foggy night shoot' on the main street bridge. I obviously snooped around the set that night, where I witnessed a car drive erratically across the bridge before speeding away into the foggy night. I decided to depart late that damp evening during a break in filming when I caught a glimpse of director Andy Muschietti alone, away from the commotion of the crew setting up the next shot. Normally hesitant about approaching people working on a film, I took advantage of the opportunity to briefly reacquaint myself with the big-time director. He

Greetings From Fairview, the fake name while filming *Welcome to Derry*, in Port Hope, Ontario

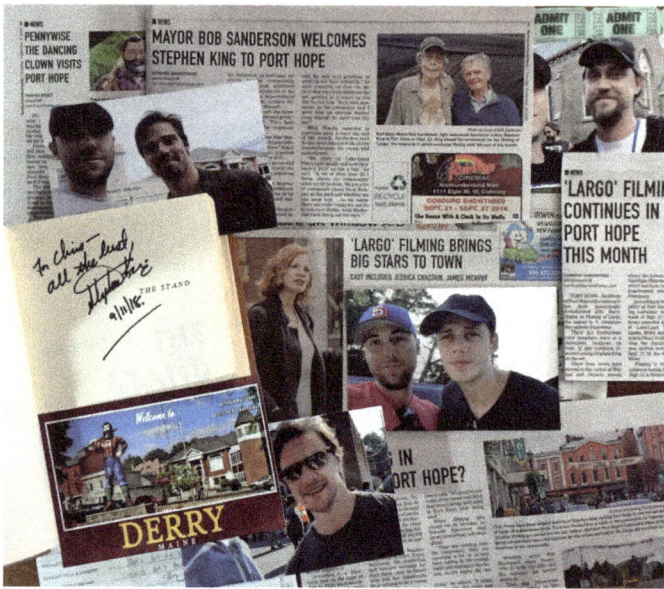

Chris Jiggins collage of his town articles, photos and featuring his Stephen King signed copy of *The Stand*.

not only remembered me from the bookstore, but after gleefully describing the extremely horrific scene they were filming, the opening of the series, he told me he wanted me in the show. He mentioned that the scene would take place in front of the bookstore and that I would need to get fitted for '60s clothes. I was conveniently costumed and fitted in town (instead of travelling to Toronto) as a bookstore owner. I then received my marching orders to show up at the background holding in a church that, as a child, I walked past on my way to school every day. I was scheduled to appear at 0930 on Thursday, April 18, 2024, for my big scene.

I waited with my fellow actors, all of whom professionally resembled small-town citizens from 1960s Maine, before walking downtown to the set. Upon arrival, I was handed a stack of Hardy Boys novels and directed by a 2 AD to step out of the bookstore onto the sidewalk, that is, until over a megaphone I heard Andy Muschietti's voice: "Chris Jiggins? Where's Chris Jiggins?" My stomach sank. Not one for the spotlight, I realized this was a big deal. Andy gave me my direction, which involved hitting my mark, then reacting to an approaching danger so that the camera could begin its elaborate move, completing a roughly twenty-second shot. Talk about pressure. I ran into Barbara, also in costume, and we got our picture taken. After my scenes,

I snuck into the bookstore on my way back to background holding to catch a glimpse of Andy directing an actor through the store's door. He even used our red balloon in the shot! Later in the day, back at my shop, cast and crew dropped in as they did throughout the shoot during breaks in the action. Later that night, I watched Andy direct the new Losers' Club bike up to the Capitol Theatre with flashlights in hand. During a break, he brought me into the tent to watch my scene before bidding me farewell with a hug. Surreal.

The only thing that remains from all three productions is the Bradley Gang mural. As of this writing, just over a month away from the series premiere, rumours swirl about a return to production in the spring. There's nothing official about a second season.

Often in the bookstore, I meet visitors who are in town to check out the filming locations and see the sites, fellow fans on a horror pilgrimage. I can relate, having made my own trek to Bangor on more than one occasion. I enjoy geeking out over anything and everything related to *IT* and Stephen King, and I don't take for granted my experiences and this ongoing opportunity to engage with a passion of mine.

I have a feeling there is much more to come.

Chris Jiggins in the doorway of Halston Hobbies, a store created for *Welcome to Derry*. In reality it's his own Furby House Books in Port Hope.

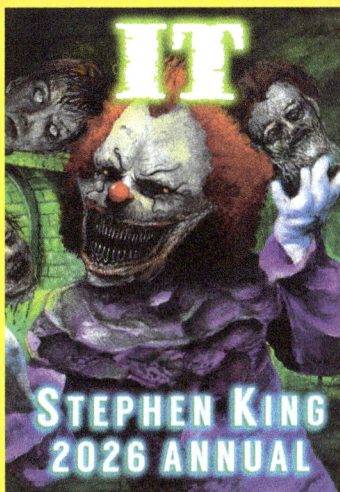

2026 STEPHEN KING ILLUSTRATED ANNUAL: *IT* 40th Anniversary

Written and Edited by Dave Hinchberger.
Cover and Interior art by Glenn Chadbourne.

▶ The Stephen King Illustrated Annual: articles, interviews, reviews, with a 52-week Calendar of Facts and Trivia! Illustrations and photos in *Full-color*!

▶ Presenting this year's theme celebrating the 40th Anniversary of Stephen King's *IT* in novel, film, and TV.

▶ *Featuring the only on set 1990 IT interview with Tim Curry!*

IT was released by Viking Press in 1986. Publisher's Weekly listed it as the best-selling book in the United States for 1986. For a novel that came in at 1,138 pages that is a lot of hardcovers to sell in one year. In 1990 *IT* became a two-part mini-series on ABC starring Tim Curry. In 2017 and 2019 *IT Chapter One* and *Chapter Two* were released in theaters and became the highest horror film franchise earning over 1.2 billion dollars world-wide, (two films combined). In October of 2025 HBO Max premieres an original story, *Welcome to Derry* in a nine-episode series. We help celebrate the 40th anniversary of the novel with this year's theme of the *2026 Stephen King Annual: IT*

▶ 2026 ANNUAL FEATURES: Award-winning artist **Glenn Chadbourne**'s original wrap-around cover features Pennywise in the sewers of Derry exclusively created for this year's Stephen King Annual and original artwork featured throughout this 250-page full-color hardcover.

▶ Introduction: *IT* Happens - **Dave Hinchberger**

▶ *BANGOR BEWARE!* How Stephen King Moved to Bangor in 1980 to Write *IT* - **Vincent Neyt**

▶ Pennywise in the flesh: **Tim Curry** Unexpurgated Interview On the Set of Stephen King's *IT* 1990. First time published in its entirety - **Steve Newton**

▶ Stephen King's *IT* – The Miniseries (1990) - **L.L. Soares**

▶ **Brandon Crane** Interview: Looks Back as **Ben Hanscom** *IT* 1990

▶ *IT* Chapters One and Two: A Representation of King's novel for the Silver Screen by **Sidney Williams**

▶ Through Blood-Tinted Glasses *IT*, Time and Again - **Kevin Quigley**

▶ The Man Behind the Mask: **Bart Mixon** - **Andrew J. Rausch**

▶ Drown Your Gays *IT* and the Art of Queer Death in Horror Fiction - **Kevin Quigley**

▶ The Supreme Compliment of My Odd Little Life by **Glenn Chadbourne**

▶ The Uglier the Better: My Love Affair with Weird King Covers - **Hans-Åke Lilja**

▶ *End of the World As We Know It: New Tales of Stephen King's The Stand*. A Review - **Tyson Blue**

▶ Stephen King and the Polish Publishing Market by **Joanna Murawska** and **Hubert Spandowski**

▶ *King Sorrow* by Joe Hill: Book Review by **Jennifer Gordon**

▶ Retro Review: *Pet Sematary* - **Kealan Patrick-Burke**

▶ Extreme King: Ultra-Rare Early Stories - **Noah Mitchell** & **Diana Petroff**

▶ 2025: A Year in Review – plus what's coming in 2026 - **Bev Vincent**

▶ 2026 Calendar: 52 Weeks of Trivia, Did You Know Facts, & Stories - **Dave Hinchberger**

Signed copies by **Dave Hinchberger** ordered at **StephenKingCatalog.com**
Trade edition is offered at **Amazon.com, BN.com**, and other retailers.
Price: 49.95   ISBN: 9781623307134   Pub Date: December, 2025

Published by **Overlook Connection Press**
PO Box 1934 Hiram, GA 30141

DECEMBER

22 MONDAY

23 TUESDAY

24 WEDNESDAY
Christmas Eve

New Stephen King Cover #19 *Christine*
available at **StephenKingCatalog.com**

"IT STARTED TO GET DARK..."

"I can remember living in Colorado, I was writing *The Stand*, the novel called *The Stand*, and we had an old American Motors car that just simply vomited up its transmission one day in the middle of the road and a tow truck came along and took it away to wherever they take, you know, transmission-less Matadors. They called around 6 or 7 o'clock after it had started to get dark, and said 'your car's ready if you want to come and get it.' My wife said, 'are you going to take a cab?' I said, 'no, I'll walk,' and I walked, and it got darker, and darker, and this was really on the edge of town, you know, there's nothing there and you can see the dealership, but it was a ways away. The path went across this bridge, you know,

DECEMBER

25 THURSDAY

Christmas Day

26 FRIDAY

Kwanzaa

27 SATURDAY

28 SUNDAY

little arched, humped- back wooden bridge. I'm walking across it, and I could hear my heels, clacking on the bridge, and I flashed to this story when I was a kid about these goats that were going across a bridge, and there's this troll underneath and said, 'who's that trip, trapping on my bridge?' And I thought, wouldn't it be a scream if something just reached out now and grabbed me and pulled me down there, and that was the last thing anybody heard of old Stevie King. So, you know, and it's funny now and I can tell you now, but I did, I ran the rest of the way across the bridge. I was like 27 or 28 years-old, but, you know, the incident stayed in my mind. Over a period of five years, I would come back to that and come back to that, little by little I began to evolve the story until now its developed into a novel that's about thirteen hundred pages long it's called *IT*, and it all came from that one little moment of fear, and I think that a moment of fear is worth having. If you can get something good out of it."

– Stephen King, University of Dayton, Ohio, March 25th, 1982

Who's that trip, trapping on my bridge?

'Salem's Lot New King cover available at StephenKingCatalog.com

21

DECEMBER

He saw himself getting up and backing away, and that was when a voice—a perfectly reasonable and rather pleasant voice–spoke to him from inside the storm drain.

"Hi, Georgie..."

– *IT*, Stephen King, Viking 1986

Art by Glenn Chadbourne

JANUARY

1 THURSDAY
New Year's Day

2 FRIDAY

3 SATURDAY

4 SUNDAY

"He did not like the cellar… because he always imagined there was something down there in the dark… while he was feeling for the light switch, some horrible clawed paw would settle lightly over his wrist... and then jerk him down into the darkness that smelled of dirt and wet and dim rotted vegetables… that cellar smell seemed to intensify until it filled the world… the smell of the monster, the apotheosis of all monsters. It was the smell of something for which he had no name: the smell of It, crouched and lurking and ready to spring."

Art by Allen Koszowski

– Stephen King, *IT*, Viking 1986

23

JANUARY

Art by Glenn Chadbourne

LET'S GET BACK... TO *IT*!

In the 1990 ABC mini-series of *IT* what song is the little girl singing as she peddles her tricycle up to her house in the very first episode? What did Mike Hanlon find at the first killing in the series next to a tree? When Mike Hanlon calls Bill Denbrough, Georgie's brother who lives in England, what does he tell Bill? Richie Tozier runs into a teacher in the cafeteria upending his food tray all over the teacher. Who is the actor that played the teacher? What series did he become famous for later and what was the character's name?

JANUARY

8 THURSDAY

9 FRIDAY

10 SATURDAY

11 SUNDAY

Answers:

A1: The Itsy Bitsy Spider

A2: A photo of Georgie, the young boy and brother of Bill Denborough that magically… appeared there.

A3: "Bill, IT's back."

A4: Actor William B. Davis played the teacher, Mr. Gedreau, in the cafeteria. He became well known as "The Smoking Man" in the *X-Files* TV series created by Chris Carter.

12 MONDAY   **13 TUESDAY**   **14 WEDNESDAY**

I'M *MAD* FOR PENNYWISE!

Tim Curry is holding an issue of *Mad* Magazine with the kids from *IT* Part 1 of the ABC mini-series. Brandon Crane, who played young Ben, said "Tim stayed focused while he was on the set, but off-set he was very warm and welcoming. There's a picture of him holding a copy of *Mad* Magazine with all of us kids floating around there to prove it." What issue of Mad Magazine is Tim Curry holding up in this photo?

IT, ABC TV mini-series 1990

15 THURSDAY

16 FRIDAY

17 SATURDAY

18 SUNDAY

Answers:

A1: Issue No. 297, September 1990, which features Alfred E. Neuman as fight manager Don King (donning Mr. King's wild hairdo), with Heavyweight boxers, Mike Tyson vs Buster Douglas on either side of Neuman.

A2: Cover artist is Mort Drucker. Mort Drucker held the longest uninterrupted tenure of any *MAD* artist for 55 years. Most of his art for *MAD* was inside the issues. He also created covers for *Time Magazine*, comics, the cover for the rock band Anthrax's album *State of Euphoria*, and most notably the movie poster for George Lucas's *American Graffiti*.

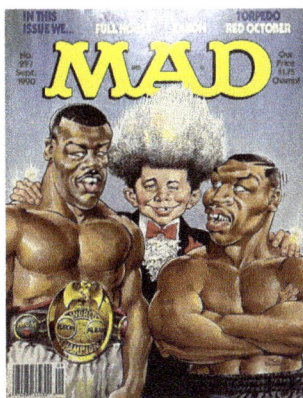

JANUARY

19 MONDAY

Martin Luther King Jr. Day

20 TUESDAY

21 WEDNESDAY

ROAD BUGS

Bill Denbrough, one of the members of The Losers' Club, now grown-up and a writer became a successful horror novelist (remind you of anyone?).

What are the titles of Bill Denbrough's novels featured in the novel, *IT*?

What are the titles of Bill Denbrough's novels featured in the *IT* ABC mini-series?

Go the extra mile and see if you remember what the tag cards read in front of two books summaries are. In the ABC mini-series, what does Richie Tozier see on the Paramount theater marquee as he drives by it in downtown Derry?

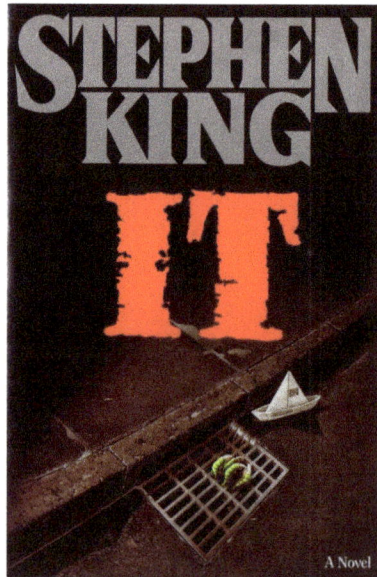

JANUARY

22 THURSDAY

23 FRIDAY

24 SATURDAY

25 SUNDAY

Answers:

A1: In the novel Bill Denbrough published the following: *The Black Rapids*. It was adapted into a film retitled as *Pit of the Black Demon* with the screenplay adapted by the author, Bill Denbrough. Stephen King has also adapted his novels into film with some success. In fact, King references in *IT* that "in spite of his agent's moans that he was insane" to also write his novels screenplay as well (agent speaking to Bill Denbrough) is most likely pulled from real-life experience with his own agent. *Attic Room* (also adapted into film). He was planning a novel he was thinking of titling *Roadbugs* (mentioned during the fortune cookie incident). He also mentions notebooks which contain the first draft of a novel titled *Joanna*, which he'd hope to publish the next year.

A2: In the ABC mini-series of *IT* they took it a little further *Highwire, Gargoyles Dance, GNAW, The Smile, The Glowing.*

A3: *Highwire*, "10,000 volts of suspense, Denbrough's all-time bestseller, set in the world of espionage." *The Glowing* tag line reads: "A vivid tale of extraterrestrial possession."

A4: Rest In Peace, Richie Tozier, Born 1950 – Died 1990. **Please note:** These are not actual books or films, but fictional items created by Stephen King for *IT*, so don't go looking for them... but just in case you do run across them in real life, don't pick it up, don't open the book... run!

IT, Richard Thomas, 1990 Lorimar Television

JANUARY

26 MONDAY   **27** TUESDAY   **28** WEDNESDAY

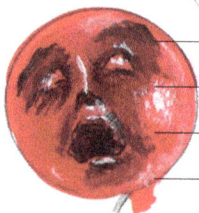

A THIN DISGUISE

You can glimpse Pennywise during the film, *Thinner*, at 14:12 right after the lawyer, Billy Halleck, hits the gypsy woman with his car. The woman was crossing the street, gets hit and tumbles over his windshield. As the windshield wiper is engaged to wipe away the blood its smeared over the windshield creating the image of Pennywise. His evil lurks, even under the surface of this moment, suggesting Pennywise caused the incident. The filmmakers purposely stay focused on the windshield as the wipers go back and forth several times so you can see that the Pennywise image is clearly inserted here. Even though smudged, you can see how during every swipe of the wipers Pennywise's image is taking shape and then

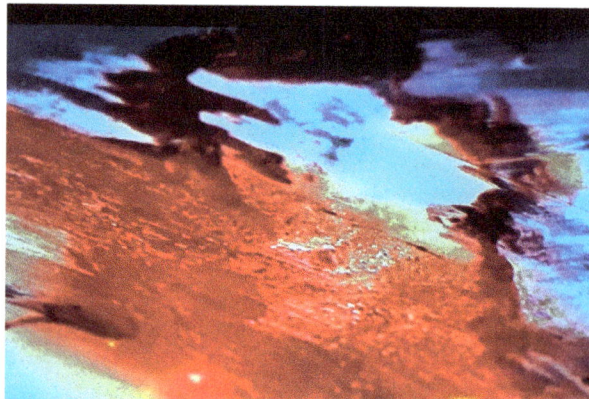

Thinner, Paramount Pictures 1996

JANUARY

29 THURSDAY

30 FRIDAY

31 SATURDAY

1 SUNDAY

wiped away. The outline of his head / hair, his eyes, his smile, it's very obvious and a cool nod to the evil one. Stephen King appears in *Thinner*. He appears in two scenes: once in the pharmacy as the pharmacist as he helps the old gypsy couple. Then the wife leaves to go to the car, crosses the street and bam! The second scene is in the courtroom where Stephen King takes the stand. In the credits he's titled as The Pharmacist, however when questioned by the judge he calls him Mr. Bangor.

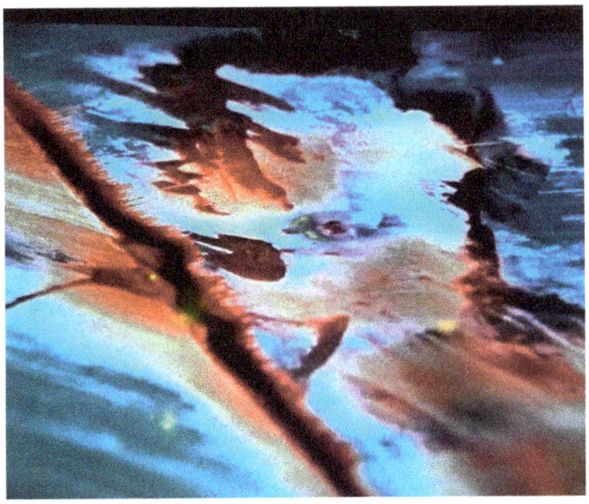

Thinner, Paramount Pictures 1996

FEBRUARY

2 MONDAY

Groundhog Day

3 TUESDAY

4 WEDNESDAY

IT – THE BEGINNINGS:

Novel and Media **THE SEED OF *IT*:** "The Three Billy Goats Gruff" is a Norwegian fairy tale about three Billy goats who try to cross a bridge to get to a lush meadow. A troll lives under the bridge and tries to stop them, but the goats outsmart him using their size and strength. This story was first published in a Norwegian collection of folk tales in 1874. Stephen King crossed a bridge in the dark one night going to retrieve his car from the repair shop. He decided to walk instead of taking a cab. He came across an oddly shaped old wooden bridge. When crossing the bridge, he heard the clap clapping of his shoes on the bridge when he thought of the story of the three Billy goats, and the

FEBRUARY

5 THURSDAY

6 FRIDAY

7 SATURDAY

8 SUNDAY

---

troll underneath. He said he ran all the way to the repair shop that he'd spooked himself so bad.

Stephen King wrote *IT* in five years.

THE ORIGINAL TITLE OF IT: *Derry.*

FIRST HARDCOVER RELEASES:

First UK Release: London, England: Hodder & Stoughton, August 1986, 912 pp. The UK released their edition one month prior to the US release.

First US Release: New York, NY: Viking, September 15th, 1986, 1138 pp.

1990 ABC TV SERIES: *IT* starring Tim Curry.

2017 Movie: *IT* (CHAPTER ONE)

2019 Movie: *IT CHAPTER TWO*

2025 HBO Series: *WELCOME TO DERRY* -- HBO Series began on October 26th, 2025, the first of eight weekly episodes.

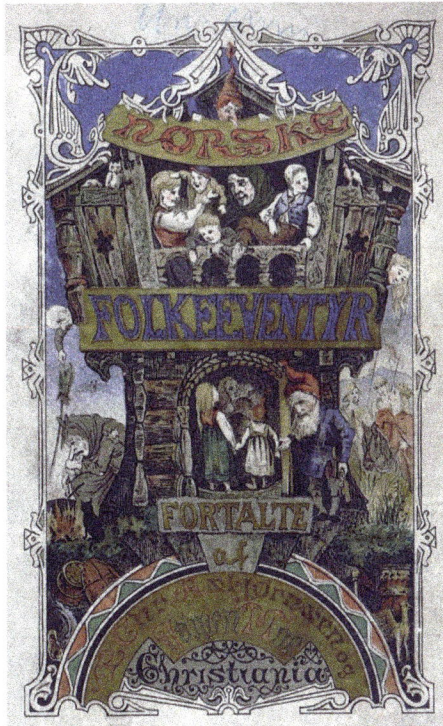

Norske Folkeeventyr, Norwegian folktales and legends by Peter Christen Asbjørnsen and Jørgen Moe. 5th edition, 1874

"...that guy under the bridge... I *still* don't know who *he* was..."

"What guy was that?" "The guy in the clown suit... The guy with the balloons."

— Stephen King, *IT*

Officer Harold Gardener has a Connection to Georgie Denbrough's death, 27 years earlier. What is it?

How old was he when this connection began? What was the name of the festival that Don Hagarty and his partner attended?

What happened to Don's partner and what was his name?

Don's partner wore a hat but angered a group of thugs. What text is featured on the hat?

Recording artist John Cougar Mellencamp is mentioned in *IT*. Why does this artist have relevance to Stephen King in years later?

What was the name of this relevance?

FEBRUARY

12 THURSDAY

13 FRIDAY

14 SATURDAY
Valentine's Day

15 SUNDAY

Answers:

A1: Harold Gardener was one of Dave Gardner's four sons. Dave had discovered Georgie's "lifeless, one-armed body" after he was killed by Pennywise.

A2: Harold was five when his father found Georgie.

A3: The Canal Days Festival.

A4: Adrian Mellon. He was killed by a gang of Derry thugs as they left the festival.

A5: the paper top-hat read: I ♠ Derry.

A5: John Cougar Mellencamp, approached Stephen King about working on a musical stage play.

A6: *The Ghost Brothers of Darkland County.*

Ghost Brothers of Darkland County CD Box Set, Concord Music Group 2013

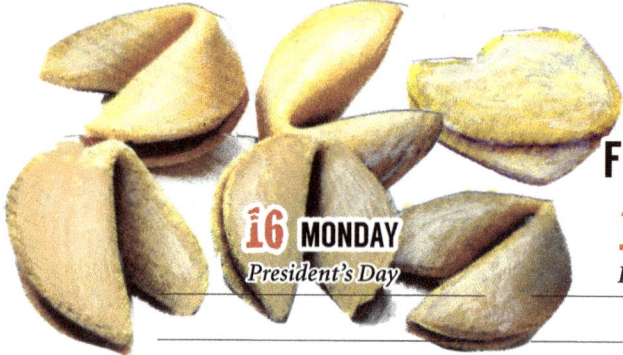

FEBRUARY

16 MONDAY
President's Day

17 TUESDAY
Lunar New Year

18 WEDNESDAY
Ash Wednesday
First Night of Ramadan

MINI-SERIES LOSERS

When The Losers' Club gets back together as adults they have dinner at a Chinese restaurant in Derry. They discover that their fortune cookies spell out a message. What is the message?

What did Stanley Uris write on the wall?

What did he use to write this message?

What movie poster is hanging in the Losers' club house, when they're kids, and when they're adults?

Photo:
Michael Edwards,
1984

FEBRUARY

19 THURSDAY

20 FRIDAY

21 SATURDAY

22 SUNDAY

Answers:

A1: "I Guess Stanley Could Not Cut It"
A2: IT
A3: he wrote "IT" using his finger with his own blood.
A4: *The Lost Boys* movie poster. It's brand new in the 80's, but 27 years later, it's still there but very weather worn.

The Lost Boys Funko Pop set, 2018 Funko Pop

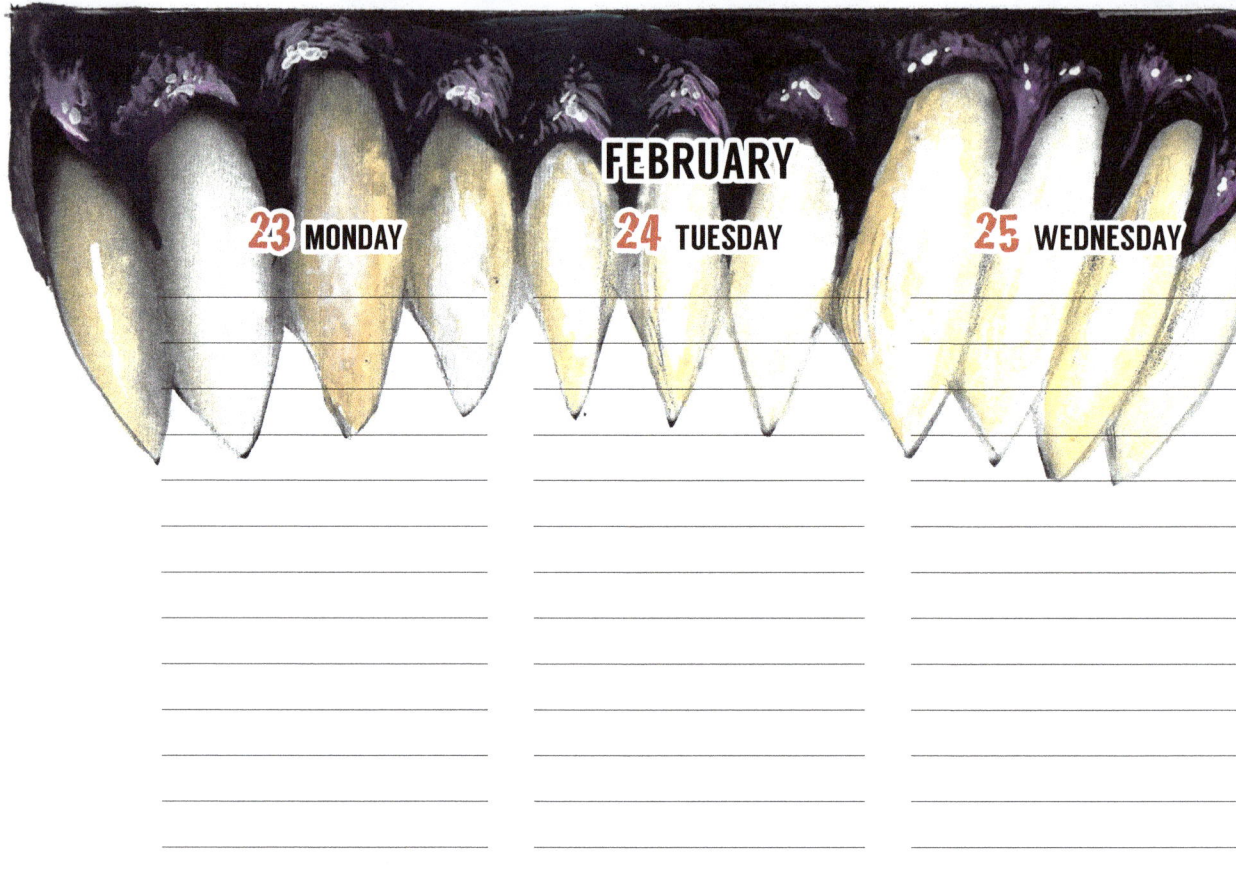

23 MONDAY   **24** TUESDAY   **25** WEDNESDAY

Glenn Chadbourne Art

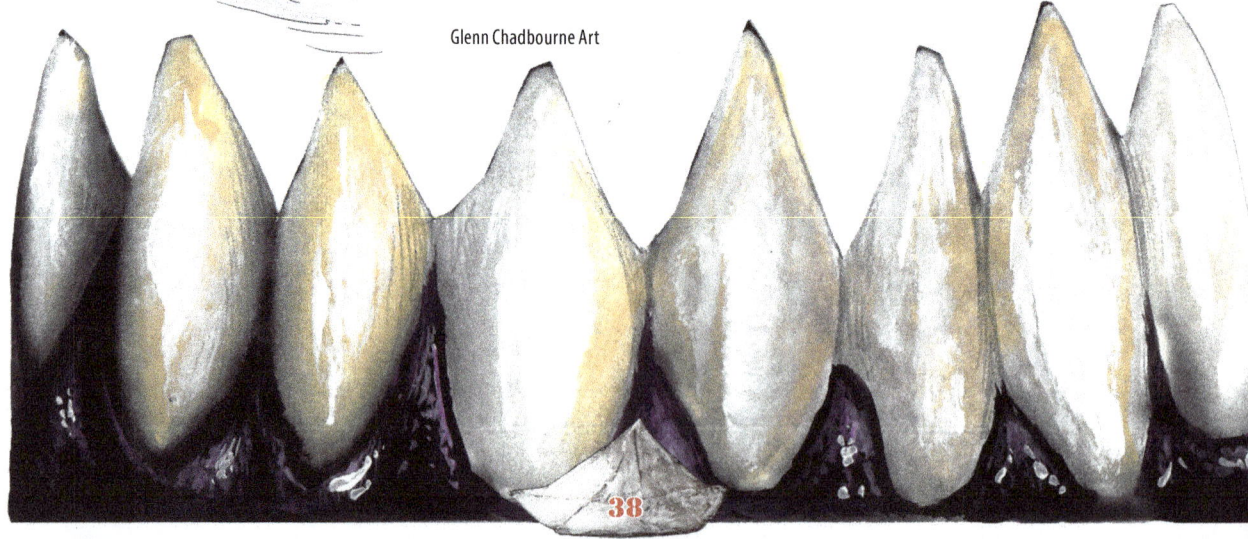

THE DAYS OF SHINOLA

As little Georgie's running down the street, he's trying to catch his waxed paper boat that's gliding in the rain created stream. He utters the words "Oh, shit and Shinola!" when it goes down the storm drain. Shinola is capitalized in the book. Do you know why? Shinola was a shoe polish and obviously something that Stephen King grew up with. Although I heard this slang many times growing up, I didn't realize it was a shoe polish. Of course, now it makes sense, from one extreme to the other: shine, and obviously the other extreme of "shit". Young Georgie's use of it truncates the original slogan which was often heard as "you don't know shit from Shinola". Georgie used this phrase in his frustration even if it's used in

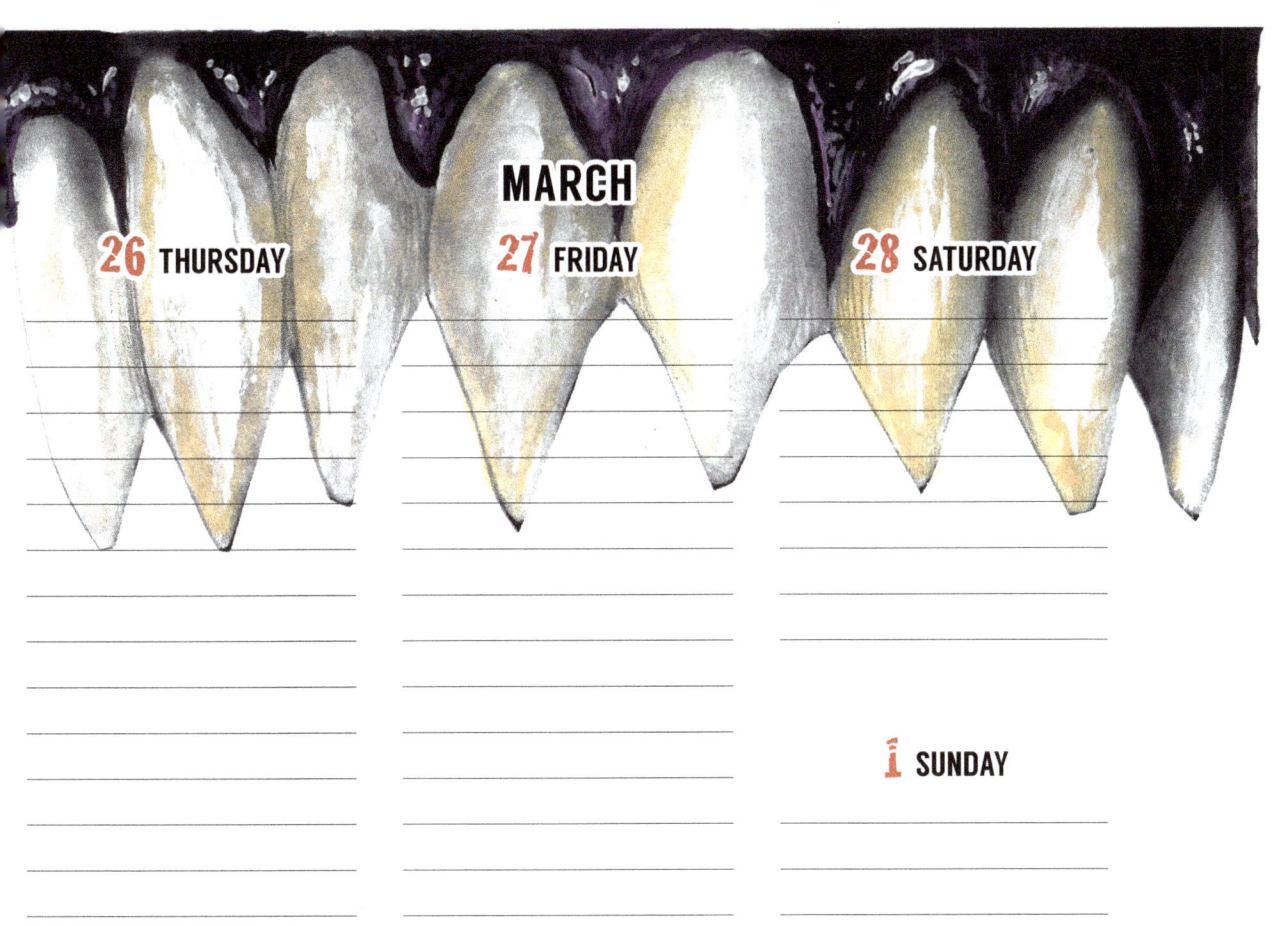

MARCH

26 THURSDAY

27 FRIDAY

28 SATURDAY

1 SUNDAY

an alternate form. Shinola is a defunct American brand of shoe polish. The Shinola Company, founded in Rochester, New York in 1877, as the American Chemical Manufacturing and Mining Company, produced the polish under a sequence of different owners until 1960. "Shinola" was a trade name and trademark for boot polish. The suffix -ola is a popular component of trade names in the United States. It was popular during the first half of the 20th century and entered the American lexicon in the phrase, "You don't know shit from Shinola," meaning to be ignorant. The brand name was acquired by the retail company Shinola in 2011. I'm in my seventh decade as I write this so I had heard this phrase a few times over the years but I probably read, or heard the slogan on from film, the slogan more often heard than said out loud. Readers in the last thirty years are probably not familiar with this slogan, but I assure you it was funny and/or shocking to some when said out loud.

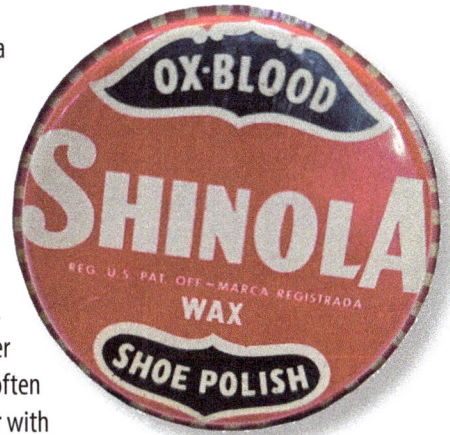

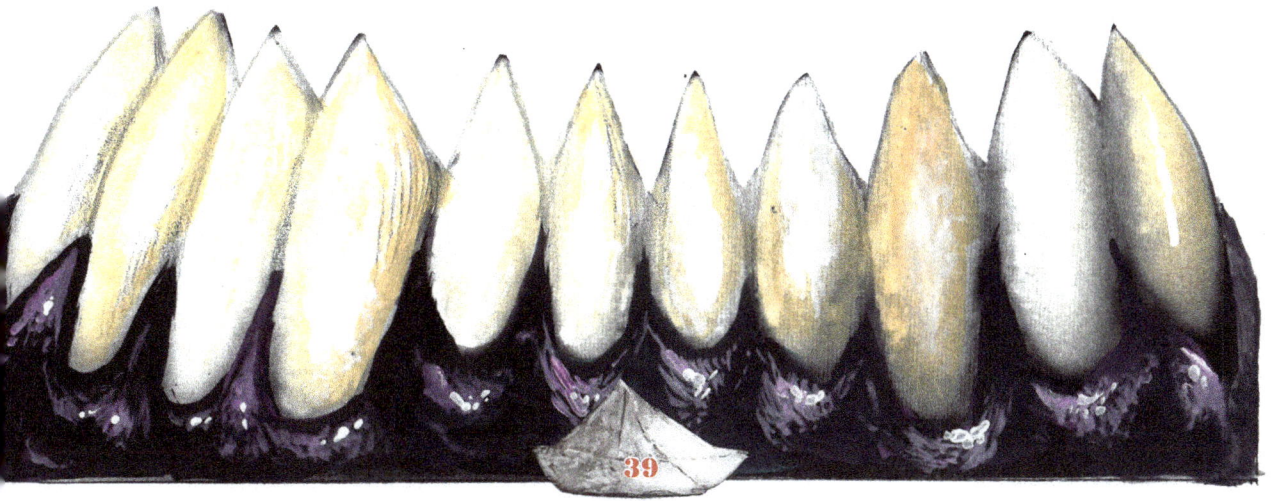

2 MONDAY

3 TUESDAY
Mardis Gras

4 WEDNESDAY
Ash Wednesday

CELLULOID TRIVIA

Who is the pharmacy customer in the aisle when Eddie Kaspbrak (*IT Chapter Two*) comes in to pick up a prescription?

What is written underneath the skateboard that slides down the stairs in the Derry (hotel?)?

When Bev is trapped in the bathroom stall, IT is trying to get in through the door in several forms. One form is Eddie Bowers. What does he say when he cracks open the door?

At the end scene in *IT Chapter Two*, when the kids are walking through town with their bikes. What is the movie listed on the marquee that is playing at the Capitol theater?

Who is Branson Buddinger?

Entertainment Weekly, July 2019

5 THURSDAY

6 FRIDAY

7 SATURDAY

8 SUNDAY
Daylight Saving begins

Answers:

A1: The director of the *IT* films, Andy Muschietti.

A2: "Won't be there for him either?"

A3: "Here's Johnny", a reference to Jack Nicholson's appearance in the Stanley Kubrick film of *The Shining*.

A4: *A Nightmare on Elm Street 5: The Dream Child* the 1989 film by Stephen Hopkins. This keeps with the time frame of the first film that it all took place originally in 1989.

A5: He is known for writing *A History of Old Derry*, which was published in 1950. The book details the town's violent history, including the 1906 Kitchener Ironworks massacre. Buddinger ultimately commits suicide, and his death is covered up by the press as an accident. The character is implied to have been driven to suicide by the entity known as IT.

IT Portfolio cover art, Glen Orbik, CD Publications

MARCH

9 MONDAY

10 TUESDAY

11 WEDNESDAY

LIFE OF CHUCK – Bangor Premiere!

with our special guest
(the man himself)
Stephen FRIGGIN' King!!
– WKIT, Bangor, Maine,
June 4th, 2025

Photos courtesy of WKIT, Bangor, Maine, 2025

WKIT 100.3 FM
2h · 🌐

We had a BLAST last night at our advanced screening of Stephen King's 'The Life of Chuck' at Bangor Mall Cinemas 10! Thanks to all of our sponsors, our lucky winners, and our special guest (the man himself) Stephen FRIGGIN' King!!

👍❤️ You + 226   5 comments 8 shares

❤️ Love   💬 Comment   📞 Send   ↪ Share

MARCH

12 THURSDAY

13 FRIDAY

14 SATURDAY

15 SUNDAY

Photos courtesy of WKIT, Bangor, Maine, 2025

11:41

Stephen King : Constant...
Jim Dexter · 3h ·

Met the man himself Wednesday night after winning tickets to the Life of Chuck premier from WKIT in Bangor. To say I was over the moon is a huge understatement!

You + 617   55 comments 1 share

Photo courtesy of Jim Dexter, 2025

16 MONDAY

17 TUESDAY
St. Patrick's Day

18 WEDNESDAY

FAST ENOUGH TO BEAT THE DEVIL

How close were you paying attention to the film of *IT Chapter Two*?

Who's the actor for the Shopkeeper of the Secondhand Rose thrift store?

What is on the t-shirt that the Seconhand Rose thrift store owner is wearing?

What book is the owner reading? How much does the antiques owner charge Bill Denbrough for the bicycle?

What other novel does Bill discover on the thrift store owner's desk?

Who is the foreword by and what is their connection to *IT*?

What is Bill's response to the thrift store owner's comment when he purchases the bike: "don't know how fast she'll go. aIt's been a lot of years."

MARCH

19 THURSDAY

_____
_____
_____
_____
_____
_____
_____
_____
_____
_____
_____
_____
_____
_____

20 FRIDAY

_____
_____
_____
_____
_____
_____
_____
_____
_____
_____
_____
_____
_____
_____

21 SATURDAY

_____
_____
_____
_____
_____

22 SUNDAY

_____
_____
_____
_____
_____

Answers:

A1: The author of *IT*, none other than Stephen King himself.

A2: Music artist Neil Young, album title *Harvest* released in 1972. It featured vocals by guests David Crosby, Graham Nash, Linda Ronstadt, Stephen Stills, and James Taylor. It topped the Billboard 200 album chart for two weeks, and spawned two hit singles, "Old Man", which peaked at No. 31 on the US Billboard Hot 100, and "Heart of Gold", which reached No. 1. It was the best-selling album of 1972 in the United States.

A3: Antiques.

A4: $300.

A5: Bill Denbrough's *The Black Rapids*, with a foreword by Jason Ballantine.

A6: Jason Ballantine. He was the film editor on *IT* and *IT Chapter Two.*

A7: Bill's response: "You know what mister? She was fast enough to beat the devil."

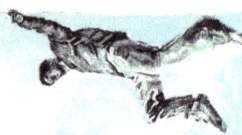

23 MONDAY

24 TUESDAY

25 WEDNESDAY

HOW *LIFE* BEGAN

The Life of Chuck, Stephen King's original novella, is the third adaptation of Stephen King's work by Mike Flanagan. *The Life of Chuck* wasn't certain to become a film however. Mike Flanagan stated in an interview in *Forbes*: "I received a manuscript before it was published," he explains. "I think a whole bunch of filmmakers did because they send it out to see who wants to grab it. I read it in April 2020, a month into the lockdown, and at a time when I was overwhelmed with anxiety and dread and felt like the world was ending. It hit too close to home for me. Initially, I didn't think I could finish reading it, but I did finish it, and by the end, I was crying with happiness, optimism, and joy, and I was so bowled over by it." "I emailed Steve that afternoon, and I said, 'I want to raise my hand on this one. I think it's gorgeous. It's one of my favorite things you've written in a very long time. If I got to do this, it might be the best film I'll ever make, so I'm here for it.' I had just gotten the rights to "The Dark Tower," and we were like, 'Let's focus on that.' Steve doesn't like you to have more than one thing,

9:25 ⁊⁊ˡ ⱽ ·

Stephen King ✓ @St... · 21h
"Magical."
"Marvelous."
"Masterpiece."

THE LIFE OF CHUCK. From the hearts and souls of Mike Flanagan and Stephen King. In Select Cities Friday, Everywhere 6.13.

It's a great movie!
(Posted at Steve King's request)

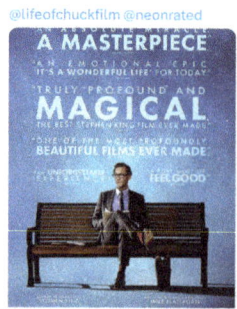

@lifeofchuckfilm @neonrated

A MASTERPIECE
AN EMOTIONAL EPIC
IT'S A WONDERFUL LIFE FOR TODAY
TRULY 'PROFOUND AND
MAGICAL
ONE OF THE MOST PROFOUNDLY
BEAUTIFUL FILMS EVER MADE

MARCH

26 THURSDAY

27 FRIDAY

28 SATURDAY

29 SUNDAY
Palm Sunday

you know, because it means one thing isn't moving, which I get. However, he said, 'I'll try to keep it warm for you. Let's see where we end up.' It would take a couple more years before I went back and said, '"The Dark Tower" is on its own timeline. It's all moving, but at its own pace, so I have time to do this. I would love to do it.' He said, Oh, in that case, 'Yeah, let's do it.'" *The Life of Chuck* premiered to rave reviews at the Toronto International Film Festival in September 2024, where it won the People's Choice Award. It opened in select theaters on Friday, June 6, 2025, then went nationwide on Friday, June 13, 2025. *The Life of Chuck* follows Charles "Chuck" Krantz, played by Tom Hiddleston, whose life is chronicled in reverse-chronological order and appears to be having an impact on the world and universe around him.

karengillan

karengillan The Life Of Chuck is out TODAY in theaters!!

Karen Gillan stars as Felicia Gordon in *The Life of Chuck*

MARCH

30 MONDAY

31 TUESDAY

1 WEDNESDAY
Passover
April Fools' Day

THAT'S *IT*!

The lyrics from "Gotta Get Next To You (Jus' Slip Me a Taste)" is written by what *IT* character? What novel does this song appear in print? The song, "Dig" is written by the fictional band Shark Puppy. What are the names of two of the band members? What novel does "Dig" appear in? As a curious aside Stephen King gives "Grateful acknowledgement" to Dennis V. Drinkwater on the copyright page of *The Girl Who Loved Tom Gordon* for reprinting lyrics. What is Drinkwater's connection to King?

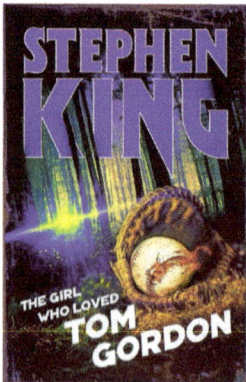

The Girl Who Loved Tom Gordon:
Halloween edition UK. Hodder & Stoughton 2019

APRIL

2 THURSDAY

_____
_____
_____
_____
_____
_____
_____
_____
_____
_____
_____
_____

3 FRIDAY
Good Friday

_____
_____
_____
_____
_____
_____

4 SATURDAY

_____
_____
_____
_____
_____
_____

5 SUNDAY
Easter

_____
_____
_____

Answers:

A1: Richie "Records" Tozier, copyright 1998 Soul Fine Music.

A2: *The Girl Who Loved Tom Gordon* by Stephen King.

A3: R. Tozier and W. Denbrough. Their full names are Richie Tozier and Bill Denbrough, both from Stephen King's novel, *IT*. Permissions to use the lyrics are from Bad Nineteen Music, copyright 1986.

A4: *Duma Key*. The opening quote of *Duma Key*, "Life is more than love and pleasure, I came to dig for treasure," is also a line from the song "Dig".

A5: King thanks Dennis Drinkwater for using the lyrics to his company's Giant Glass commercial jingle. Their connection was formed by being Red Sox season tickets fans sitting behind home plate. Drinkwater is on the front row, and Stephen King is on the second row at the Red Sox games. Both are considered two of the team's biggest fans.

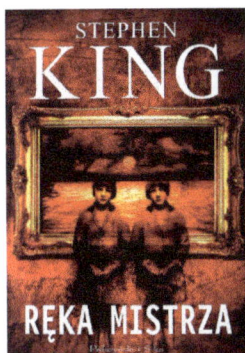

Duma Key Poland edition,
PrÄlszyŁski i S-ka 2008

APRIL

6 MONDAY

7 TUESDAY

8 WEDNESDAY

ALLIGATORS IN THE SEWER

Exterior of the sewer set in *IT* (2017). Much of the sewer's design was built, with real water flowing through sections of the set to create a sense of authenticity. The art department constructed detailed tunnels and chambers, complete with rusted pipes, grimy textures, and flickering lighting to evoke a claustrophobic and eerie atmosphere. One of the most notable parts of the set was Pennywise's lair, where the Losers' Club confronts the clown. This space was filled with props such as discarded children's toys, floating debris, and the iconic mountain of junk and bodies. The filmmakers relied on a mix of these physical elements and minimal CGI to ensure the actors could interact with their environment, enhancing the realism of their performances. The attention to detail in the practical set helped bring the terrifying world of Derry's sewers to life.

APRIL

9 THURSDAY

10 FRIDAY

11 SATURDAY

12 SUNDAY

IT Sewer: From the set of *IT* (2017) the outside structure of the sewer from the film. Warner Bros, 2017

POPPIN' WITH PENNYWISE!

IT: Pennywise Exclusive Popcorn Bucket. Turn your movie nights into a thrilling experience with the *IT*: Pennywise Popcorn Bucket! Featuring a hauntingly detailed design of the infamous Pennywise, this collectible bucket is perfect for fans of the horror classic. Snack in spooky style and show off your love for *IT*! This beautiful popcorn bucket was created for *IT Chapter Two* and exclusively available at Cinemark theaters. I was surprised that IT. . . is still available to order at their website.

- Measures 9.1" x 6.7" x 9.1"
- Plastic
- Hand wash only
- Available at shop.cinemark.com

2019 Cinemark *IT Chapter Two* popcorn bucket

16 THURSDAY   **17** FRIDAY   **18** SATURDAY

19 SUNDAY

PENNYWISE IN OZ

Hoyts Limited Promotional Pennywise Popcorn Bucket for *IT Chapter Two*.

Hoyts cinemas in Australia (affectionately known as OZ), created this unique limited edition popcorn bucket in 2019 to celebrate the chilling return of Pennywise *IT Chapter Two* to the theaters there.

Designed exclusively for the promotional theatre release, this collectible combined practical use with iconic horror imagery. Perfect for fans and collectors, it offers a unique way to enjoy your movie snacks while showcasing your passion for the franchise.

Collectors can find this on Ebay.

2019 Hoyts *IT Chapter Two* popcorn bucket

Holly

You Like it Darker

Sleeping Beauties Wraparound Cover

The Shining

A NEW and ORIGINAL COVER FOR EVERY STEPHEN KING BOOK !

The New Stephen King Cover Series is an ongoing project of original paintings based on all Stephen King novels and collections. These original wraparound dust jacket covers are a signed limited series by acclaimed Stephen King artist, Glenn Chadbourne. All Covers are Signed by the Artist! See All Covers at StephenKingCatalog.com under Glenn Chadbourne Category

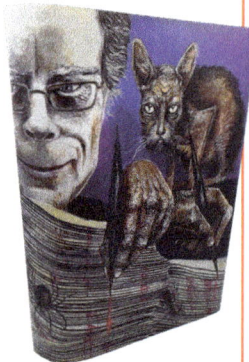
If It Bleeds

The Stand

Fairy Tale

STEPHEN KING
HEARTS IN SUSPENSION
WITH ESSAYS BY COLLEGE CLASSMATES AND FRIENDS

STEPHEN KING
HEARTS IN SUSPENSION

THE UNIVERSITY OF MAINE PRESS

Civil

HEARTS IN SUSPENSION:

STEPHEN KING REMEMBERS A LOST ATLANTIS

This publication marks the 50th anniversary of Stephen King's entrance into the University of Maine at Orono in the fall of 1966. The accelerating war in Vietnam and great social upheaval at home exerted a profound impact on students of the period and deeply influenced King's development as a writer and as a man.

Features in *Hearts In Suspension*:

- Stephen King's original story of this experience in his novella "Hearts in Atlantis" is published here.

- In his accompanying essay, "Five to One, One in Five," written expressly for this volume, King sheds his fictional persona and takes on the challenge of a nonfiction return to his undergraduate experience.

- Twelve fellow students and friends from King's college days contribute personal narratives recalling their own experience of those years.

- This book also includes four installments of King's never-before-reprinted student newspaper column, "King's Garbage Truck." These lively examples of King's damn-the-torpedoes style, entertaining and shrewd in their youthful perceptions, more than hint at a talent about to take its place in the American literary landscape.

- A gallery of period photographs and documents augments this volume.

Hearts In Suspension is a unique and one-of-a-kind Stephen King publication.

First printing hardcover available at StephenKingCatalog.com

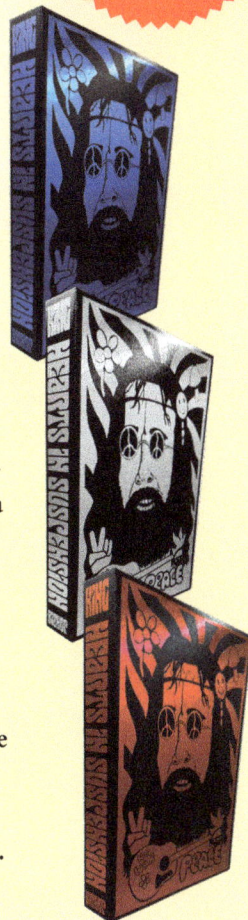

APRIL

20 MONDAY

21 TUESDAY

22 WEDNESDAY
Earth Day

WHAT IS *IT*?

Not only has Stephen King been a contestant on Jeopardy but he has been a "category" on a few episodes. In one episode the following was a $200 question and was asked: "The title entity of IT appears in many different forms, including as Pennywise, one of these circus performers."

THE TITLE ENTITY OF "IT" APPEARS IN MANY DIFFERENT FORMS, INCLUDING AS PENNYWISE, ONE OF THESE CIRCUS PERFORMERS

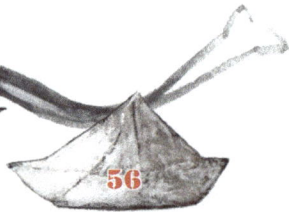

23 THURSDAY

24 FRIDAY

25 SATURDAY

26 SUNDAY

In a different episode: This Stephen King novel says, "I, Georgie, am Mr. Bob Gray, also known as Pennywise the Dancing Clown."
What are the answers?

Answers:

A2: "What is *IT*."

A1: "What is a clown" was the answer given by the contestant. Dancing clown would also have been valid.

THIS STEPHEN KING NOVEL SAYS, "I, GEORGIE, AM MR. BOB GRAY, ALSO KNOWN AS PENNYWISE THE DANCING CLOWN"

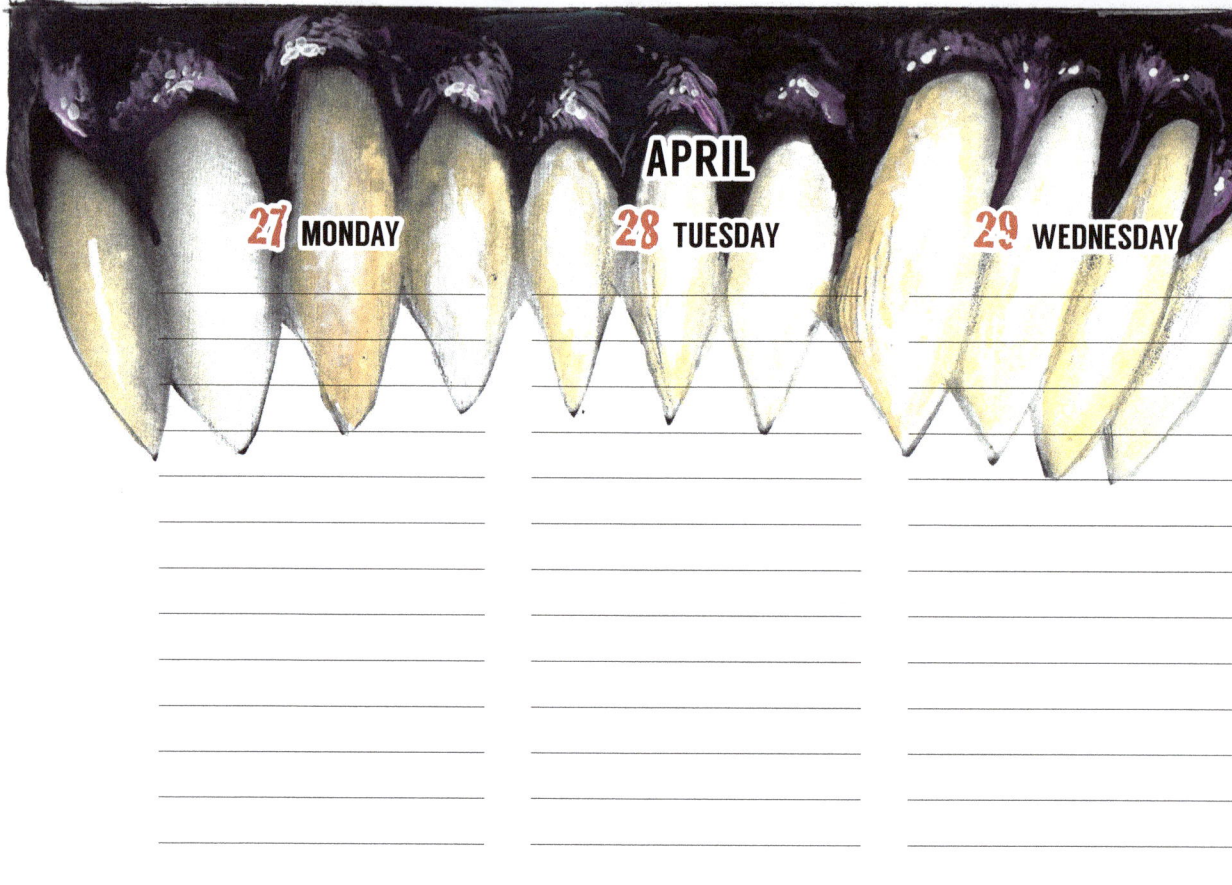

27 MONDAY

28 TUESDAY

29 WEDNESDAY

INSPIRATION FOR *IT*

In 1978 my family was living in Boulder, Colorado. One day on our way back from lunch at a pizza emporium, our brand-new AMC Matador dropped its transmission-literally. The damn thing fell out on Pearl Street. True embarrassment is standing in the middle of a busy downtown street, grinning idiotically while people examine your marooned car and the large greasy black thing lying under it. Two days later the dealership called at about five in the afternoon. Everything was jake–I could pick up the car any time. The dealership was three miles away. I thought about calling a cab but decided that the walk would be good for me. The AMC dealership was in an industrial park

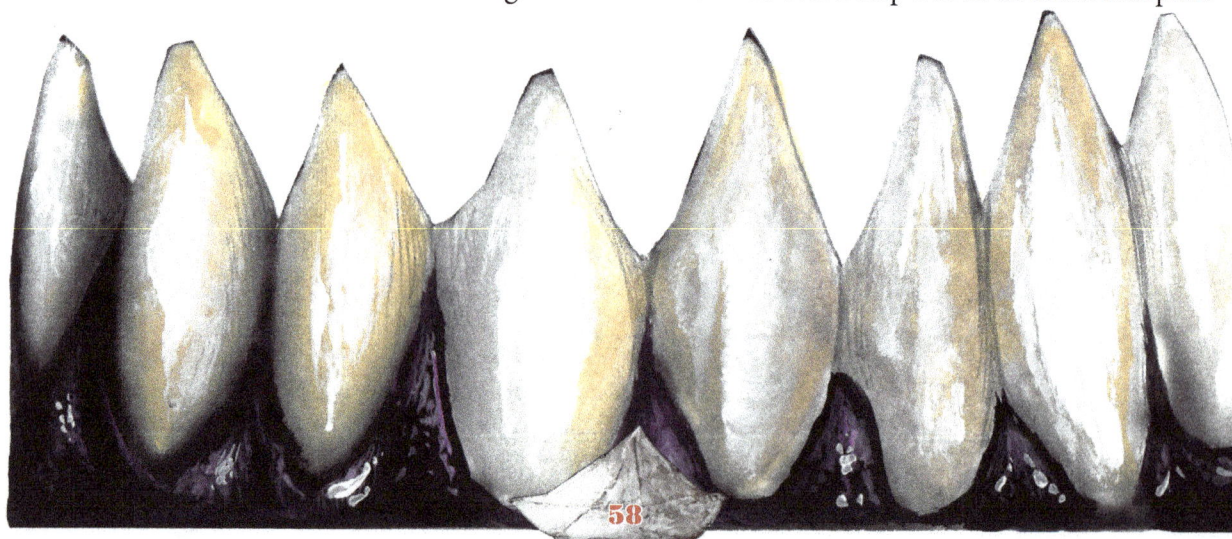

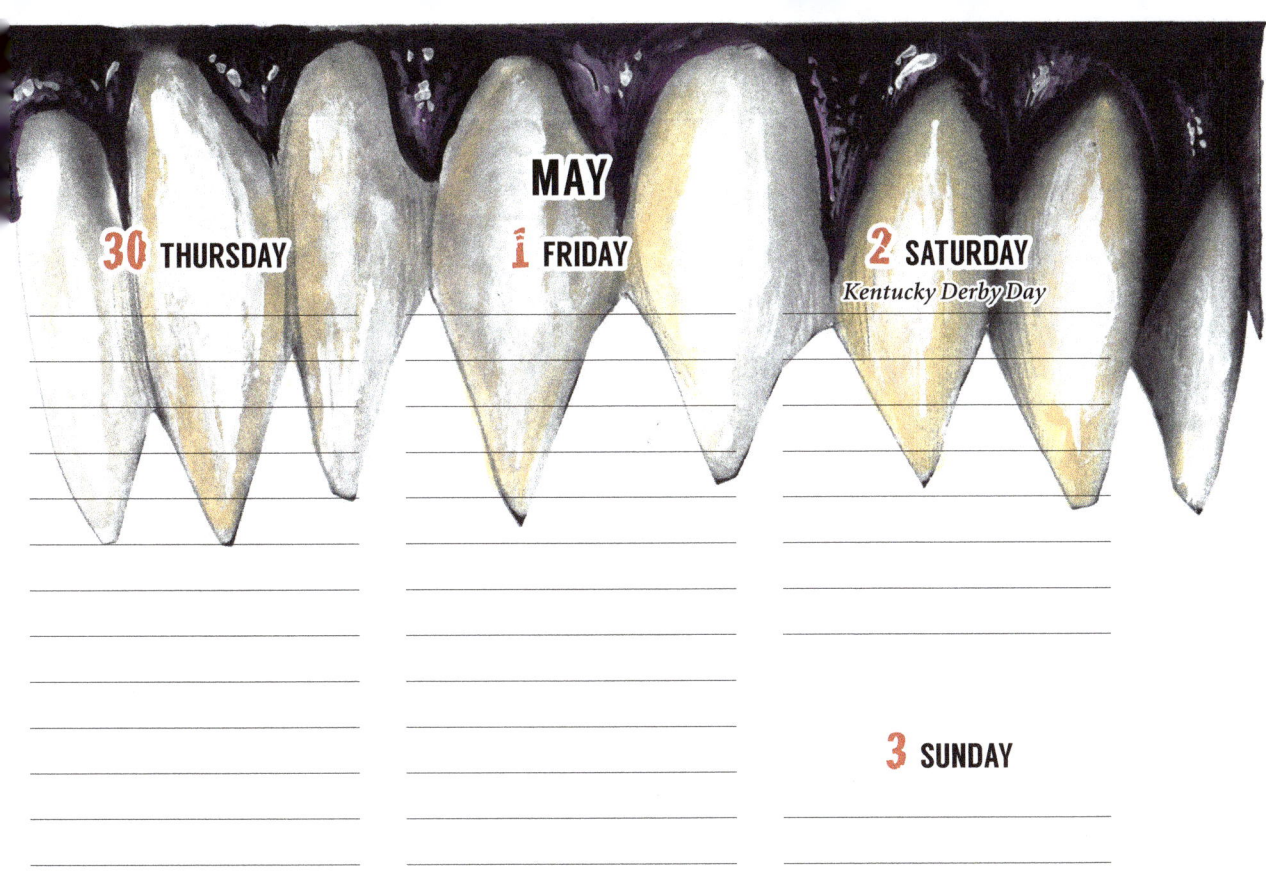

MAY

30 THURSDAY

1 FRIDAY

2 SATURDAY
Kentucky Derby Day

3 SUNDAY

set off by itself on a patch of otherwise deserted land a mile from the strip of fast-food joints and gas stations that mark the eastern edge of Boulder. A narrow unlit road led to this outpost. By the time I got to the road it was twilight–in the mountains the end of day comes in a hurry–and I was aware of how alone I was. About a quarter of a mile along this road was a wooden bridge, humped and oddly quaint, spanning a stream. I walked across it. I was wearing cowboy boots with rundown heels, and I was very aware of the

Art by Allen Koszowski, 1990

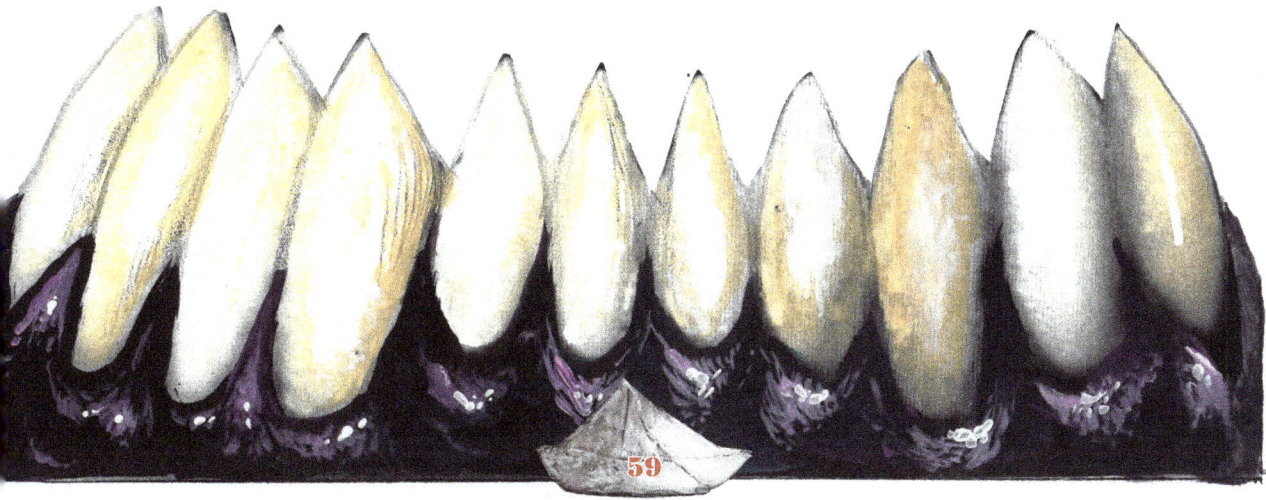

sound they made on the boards; they sounded like a hollow clock. I thought of the fairy tale called "The Three Billy-Goats Gruff" and wondered what I would do if a troll called out from beneath me, "Who is trip-trapping upon my bridge?" All of a sudden I wanted to write a novel about a real troll under a real bridge. I stopped, thinking of a line by Marianne Moore, something about "real

MAY

4 MONDAY

5 TUESDAY
Cinco de Mayo

6 WEDNESDAY

_____

toads in imaginary gardens," only it came out "real trolls in imaginary gardens." A good idea is like a yo-yo–it may go to the end of its string, but it doesn't die there; it only sleeps. Eventually it rolls back up into your palm. I forgot about the bridge and the troll in the business of picking up my car and signing the papers, but it came back to me off and on over the next two years. I decided that the bridge could be some sort of symbol–a point of passing. I started thinking of Bangor, where I had lived, with its strange canal bisecting the city, and decided that the bridge could be the city, if there was something under it. What's under a city? Tunnels. Sewers.

Glenn Chadbourne Art, 2016

Ah! What a good place for a troll! Trolls should live in sewers! A year passed. The yo-yo stayed down at the end of its string, sleeping, and then it came back up. I started to remember Stratford, Connecticut, where I had lived for

60

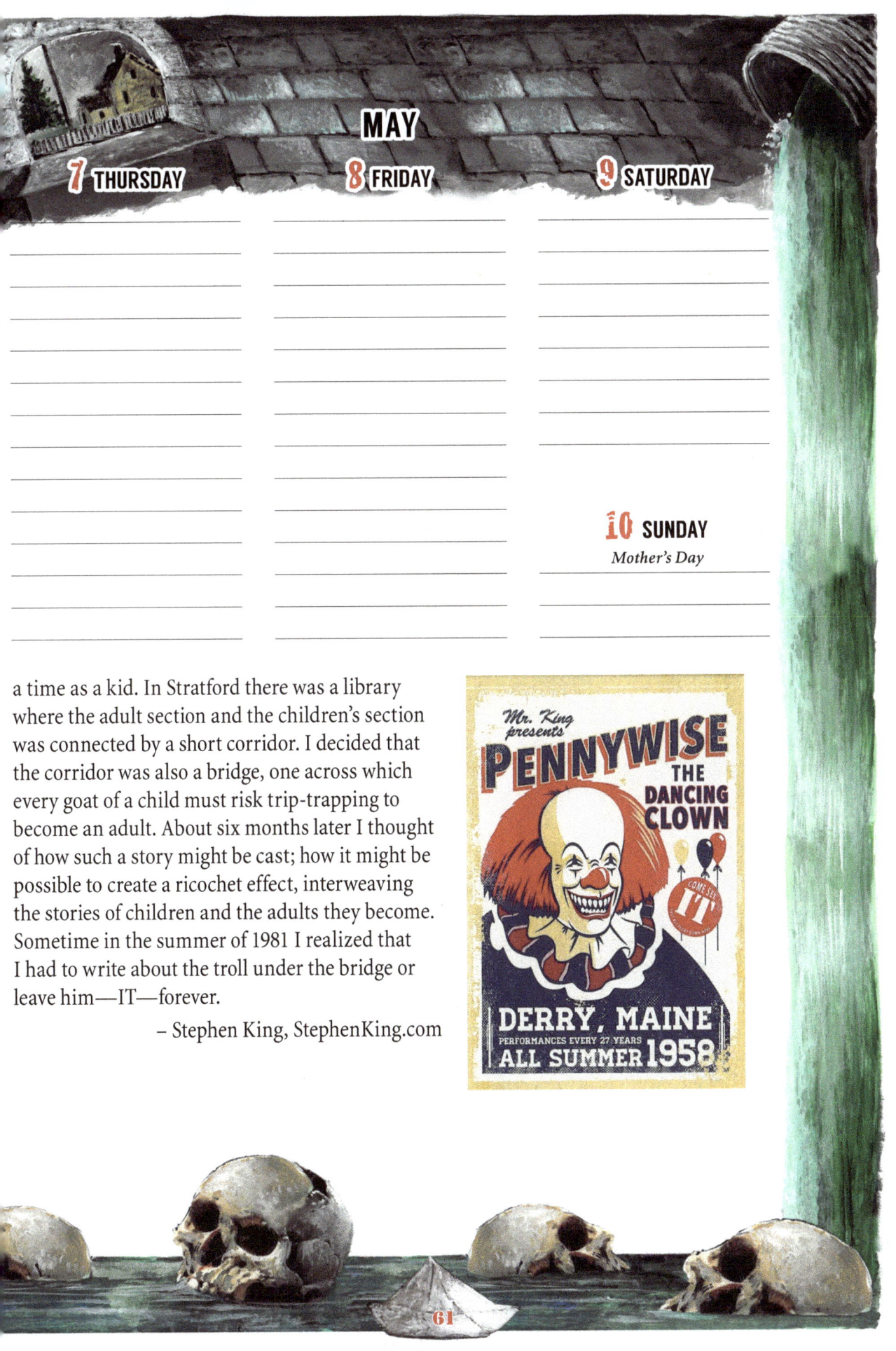

MAY

7 THURSDAY

8 FRIDAY

9 SATURDAY

10 SUNDAY
Mother's Day

a time as a kid. In Stratford there was a library where the adult section and the children's section was connected by a short corridor. I decided that the corridor was also a bridge, one across which every goat of a child must risk trip-trapping to become an adult. About six months later I thought of how such a story might be cast; how it might be possible to create a ricochet effect, interweaving the stories of children and the adults they become. Sometime in the summer of 1981 I realized that I had to write about the troll under the bridge or leave him—IT—forever.

– Stephen King, StephenKing.com

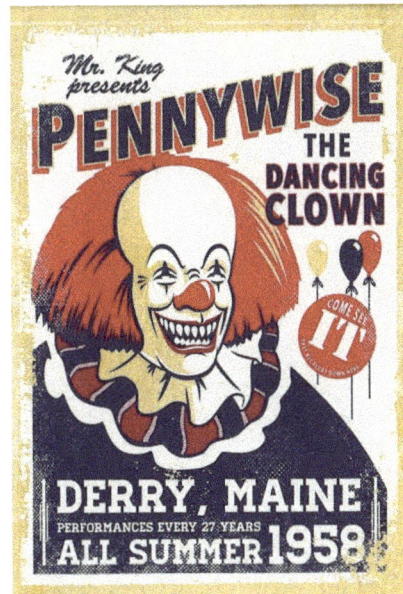

Mr. King presents'
PENNYWISE
THE DANCING CLOWN
COME SEE IT

DERRY, MAINE
PERFORMANCES EVERY 27 YEARS
ALL SUMMER 1958

MAY

11 MONDAY

_____
_____
_____
_____
_____
_____
_____
_____
_____
_____
_____
_____

12 TUESDAY

_____
_____
_____
_____
_____
_____
_____
_____
_____
_____
_____
_____

13 WEDNESDAY

_____
_____
_____
_____
_____
_____
_____
_____
_____
_____
_____
_____

Art by Allen Koszowski

SUBMISSION

What is the name of the story that Bill Denborough has written in a "white heat" until four in the morning?

What is this story about?

What does the story have in common with the novel _IT_?

Where does Bill Denbrough submit the story?

How does this story, and his submission, have a historic connection with Stephen King?

MAY

14 THURSDAY

15 FRIDAY

16 SATURDAY

17 SUNDAY

Answers:

Which is exactly what Stephen King did to get published in the early 70's, and it worked!

A5: In the 70's, Stephen King had several stories published in men's magazines, now collector's items. As this is exactly what happened to him he gives a look into his own personal story in that the *Writer's Market* magazine "says they buy horror stories," he bought two issues at a local convenience store "and have indeed contained four horror stories sandwiched between the naked girls and the ads for dirty movies and potency pills."

A4: *White Tie*, a men's adult magazine.

A3: As the description above states, it's basically the story of *IT* defeated by one boy, not a group like The Losers' Club in the novel. The premise is the same.

A2: *IT*'s "a tale about a small boy who discovers a monster in the cellar of his house. The little boy faces it, battles it, finally kills it."

A1: "The Dark", a short story that is a "fifteen-page sheaf of manuscript".

Cavalier Magazine, December 1972

This issue of *Cavalier* features the first publication of Stephen King's "The Mangler"

18 MONDAY

19 TUESDAY

20 WEDNESDAY

Glenn Chadbourne Art

"When you're down here with me, you'll float too!"

Vancouver filming locations of the 1990s *IT* miniseries. Areas of metro Vancouver was transformed into the fictional 1960s town of Derry, Maine, for the 1990 ABC miniseries of *IT*. If you're from the Vancouver area then you'll be slightly more unnerved to learn that line was delivered in the Metro Vancouver area. If that doesn't get to you then know it was delivered by none-other than Tim Curry himself, the man who's offered up one of the best portrayals of the demonic, shape-shifting, child-crunching clown, Pennywise. The scene where the line is delivered serves as the titular villain's introduction in the 1990s miniseries based on Stephen King's *It*. Georgie Denbrough was chasing his paper boat down a river of rainwater which led to a storm drain on

MAY

21 THURSDAY

22 FRIDAY

23 SATURDAY

24 SUNDAY

Sewer drain used in IT from the film, and in 2021. A separate set was created for Pennywise to peer from the sewer to Georgie.

3rd Street in New Westminster. It was at that drain, which has since been upgraded, where Georgie had his fatal meeting with the ominous Pennywise the clown. Many scenes from the miniseries have been well documented and posted in videos uploaded to YouTube in the last few years. Shot over a three-month period, *It*'s filming locations included Stanley Park, Beaver Lake and Saint Thomas Aquinas High School Convent in North Vancouver. The Buntzen Lake Hydro Plant was used as the miniseries' sewer plant. The miniseries turns Metro Vancouver into the fictional town of Derry, Maine in the 1960s then once more when Pennywise returns in the 1990s.

– Cameron Thomson

25 MONDAY
Memorial Day

26 TUESDAY

27 WEDNESDAY

DEAD END KID

Who is the actor who plays Henry Bowers as an adult in the 1990 *IT* ABC miniseries?

He made quite a splash in a TV series in the late 60's and early 70's. Name the show.

A famous actress played Bill Denbrough's wife in the 1990 *IT* ABC miniseries. Who is she?

What film brought her world-wide attention in the sixties?

What popular horror film in 1974 did she also appear in?

She also appeared in what Mick Garris horror film in 1990? Mick Garris who is known for directing *The Stand*, *The Shining*, *Sleepwalkers*, and many more Stephen King productions. Why is this trivia segment titled the Dead End Kid?

The Mod Squad, Michael Cole, ABC TV 1973

MAY

28 THURSDAY

29 FRIDAY

30 SATURDAY

_____
_____
_____
_____
_____
_____
_____
_____
_____
_____
_____
_____
_____
_____

31 SUNDAY

Answers:

A1: Michael Cole played Henry Bowers in Stephen King's original miniseries *It* (1990), as a vicious bully who does the bidding of the shapeshifting entity, Pennywise.

Michael Cole (July 3, 1940 – December 10, 2024).

A2: Michael Cole was best known for his role as Pete Cochran on *The Mod Squad* (1968-1973), a big hit from ABC television.

A3: Olivia Hussey.

A4: She was Juliet in Franco Zeffirelli's 1968 film adaptation of *Romeo and Juliet*.

A5: In 1974, she appeared in the cult slasher film *Black Christmas*.

A6: She appeared alongside Anthony Perkins in the 1990 film, *Psycho IV: The Beginning*.

A7: I'm stretching here but I just couldn't shake it, so I used it. *The Bowery Boys* were the subject of 48 films in the 40's and 50's. The group originated as the *Dead End Kids* in the 1937 film *Dead End*. Since Henry has the last name of "Bower" and he eventually ended up as a "dead end kid" I thought this was a fun reference.

Michael Cole as Henry Bowers in *IT*. ABC miniseries 1990

JUNE

TRIVIA: *IT: CHAPTER TWO*

What is the name of the book by William Denbrough sitting on the desk next to his computer? What is the title of the film they're shooting with them in the beginning of *IT Chapter Two*? Who is the director of this film within *IT Chapter Two*? Hint it's a cameo by a very famous director and one of his last roles as an actor.

IT Chapter Two 4K Ultra HD Zavvi Exclusive Ultimate Collector's Edition, 2020 Warner Brothers. Ebay.com

68

JUNE

4 THURSDAY

_____
_____
_____
_____
_____
_____
_____
_____
_____
_____
_____
_____

5 FRIDAY

_____
_____
_____
_____
_____
_____
_____
_____
_____
_____
_____
_____

6 SATURDAY

7 SUNDAY

Answers:

A1: *The Attic Room.*

A2: This one is tricky. The back of the director's chairs that are sitting on the set read *The Attic Room.* However, on the camera casing that is next to the director (who's sitting) it reads *Attic Panic,* which we'll assume is the changed titled for the film version of *The Attic Room.* In this case either answer is correct.

A3: Peter Bogdanovich. In fact, during the film set scene when the wife/actress is talking she refers to the director as "Peter". Peter Bogdanovich made many memorable films over his career including the director of Academy nominated films, *The Last Picture Show,* and *Paper Moon.* He was a film historian and a student of director Alfred Hitchcock.

IT Chapter Two, advance poster, Warner Bros. 2019

JUNE

8 MONDAY   **9** TUESDAY   **10** WEDNESDAY

CHAPTER TWO APPEARANCES

IT: Chapter Two. At 1:17:20 - The Shopkeeper, Stephen King's cameo, sits behind his desk at the Secondhand Rose thrift store when Bill Denbrough comes in. Did you notice the small cup that Stephen King has, the one he sips out of with a straw? This is a unique cup. As a nod to *IT* director Andy Muschietti – who is Argentinian – Stephen King is shown drinking yerba mate, an Argentinian tea, out of a mate, the traditional urn-like cup. Emblazoned with the Club Atlético Independiente crest. That's the team Andy Muschietti supports from his homeland and the mate was given to

Stephen King cameo, *IT Chapter Two,* Warner Bros. 2019

him by a fan. In the same scene did you by chance notice the yellow license plate above the shopkeeper at his desk? It reads "CQB 241" on a California license plate from the 1983 movie *Christine* (based on Stephen King's novel), where the car is known as "CQB 241". "CQB" stands for "close quarters battle," which describes Christine's method of attack, while the "241" is a cryptic reference to Arnie's victims

JUNE

11 THURSDAY

_____
_____
_____
_____
_____
_____
_____
_____
_____
_____
_____

12 FRIDAY

_____
_____
_____
_____
_____
_____
_____
_____
_____
_____
_____

13 SATURDAY

_____
_____
_____
_____
_____
_____

14 SUNDAY
Flag Day

_____
_____
_____

getting a "two for one." At 1:25 in the film, a large Turtle, a nod to Maturin, shows up on the desk at Derry High School when Ben, as an adult, goes by to visit. At 1:26 in the film, the filmmakers take us back in time in the same class room where young Ben is left sitting alone as the students exit. The room is dark, with the curtains drawn, with the projector showing a Chinese Dragon on the screen. What do you see spelled out in the curtains next to it? Go take a look, I'll wait. Obviously done on purpose the curtains are altered just enough to let the light in to spell out "IT". Cool huh? Makes me wonder where else _IT_ shows up in the films. I'll keep looking. You let me know if you find more appearances.

Club Atlético Independiente Argentinian
official football team crest

15 MONDAY   **16** TUESDAY   **17** WEDNESDAY

DID YOU KNOW?

In *IT Chapter Two*, Bill Denbrough ends up in the pawn shop owned by Stephen King's character, aka the "Shopkeeper" while looking for his childhood bicycle, Silver, which he sees displayed in the shop window. Originally though, Bill had a flashback scene while in the thrift shop, reliving a potential tender moment between he and Bev as kids. This moment would've been interrupted by a younger version of Stephen King's Shopkeeper.

CALIFORNIA **56**
CQB 241

The license plate for *Christine* that is hung up in the Secondhand Rose store.

21 SUNDAY
Father's Day

Director Andy Muschietti planned to cast Stephen King's own son and fellow author, Joe Hill, as the young shopkeeper. Wouldn't that have been a cool scene!? Joe Hill is the spitting image of his father at the same age. Unfortunately, the script was deemed too long, and the flashback portion of King and Hill's cameo was cut for time. Damn.

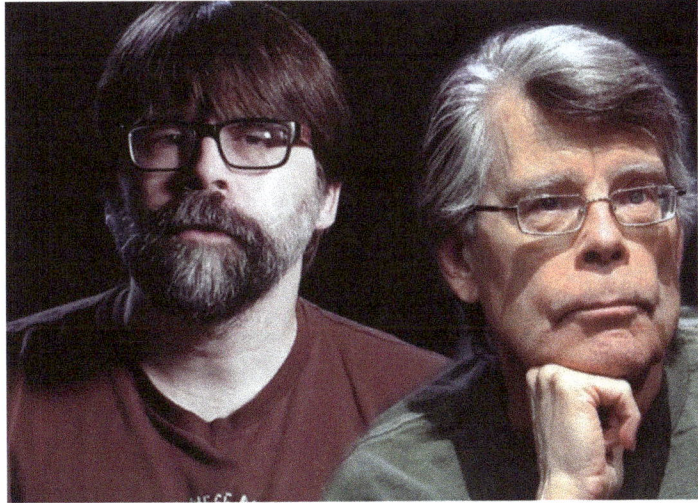

Joe Hill and Stephen King

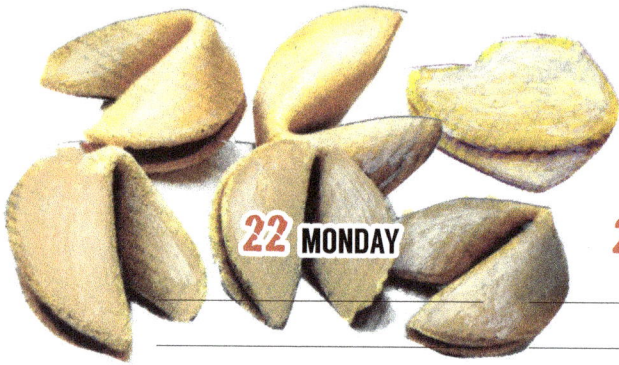

JUNE

22 MONDAY   **23 TUESDAY**   **24 WEDNESDAY**

ROMERO'S *IT*

"I had written *Carrie*, and that had put Steve King, Brian de Palma, the actors, and me on the map in a way that I became a go to for horror adaptations. I got a call one day from my agent in Los Angeles, who said, he'd been approached by a pair of producers who set up a new Stephen King project at ABC as a novel for television, and was I interested in that. The next day the doorbell rang, Federal Express at the door, and the guy is carrying the most humongous FedEx package I've ever seen. I took this unwieldy bulky piece from him and was about to close the door and he said, "hang on a minute" and he went back to the elevator and came back with these two giant containers containing the typed manuscript of *IT* in its earliest stages. I sat down and read the

"IT"

(ABC Miniseries)

———

Based on the Novel
by STEPHEN KING

———

Story Outline
By
LAWRENCE D. COHEN

Pennywise: The Story of IT, 2021
Courtesy of John Campopiano

JUNE

25 THURSDAY

26 FRIDAY

27 SATURDAY

_____
_____
_____
_____
_____
_____
_____
_____
_____
_____
_____
_____
_____

28 SUNDAY

opening with young stuttering Bill, and baby brother Georgie, turns out to be a horrible demise at the hands of Pennywise, in the sewer. I went, 'I'll do it.' We went in for a first reading with the network and the executive Vice President of movies for television, and she looked at me and she said, 'so tell me, what is IT?' and I said, 'well, it's an Intraterrestrial beast that has come down eons ago, and has the power to screw with kids' minds and attack their worst fears.' And she looked at me, she nodded, and she said, 'yes, but what is IT?' and I answered another answer, and she asked me, I don't know, five more times and I looked over at the producers and went, 'I'm in hell.' I was coming back home to New York. I'm sitting on the plane

and I see a guy with his back to me reading what is clearly the cover of my script. It's Bob Iger, who was the head of all the programming at ABC, and he whipped through night one, went to his briefcase, pulled out night two, whipped

Molly Ranson (Carrie), composer Michael Gore, book and screenwriter Lawrence D. Cohen, Marin Mazzie (Margaret White)

75

JUNE

29 MONDAY

30 TUESDAY

1 WEDNESDAY

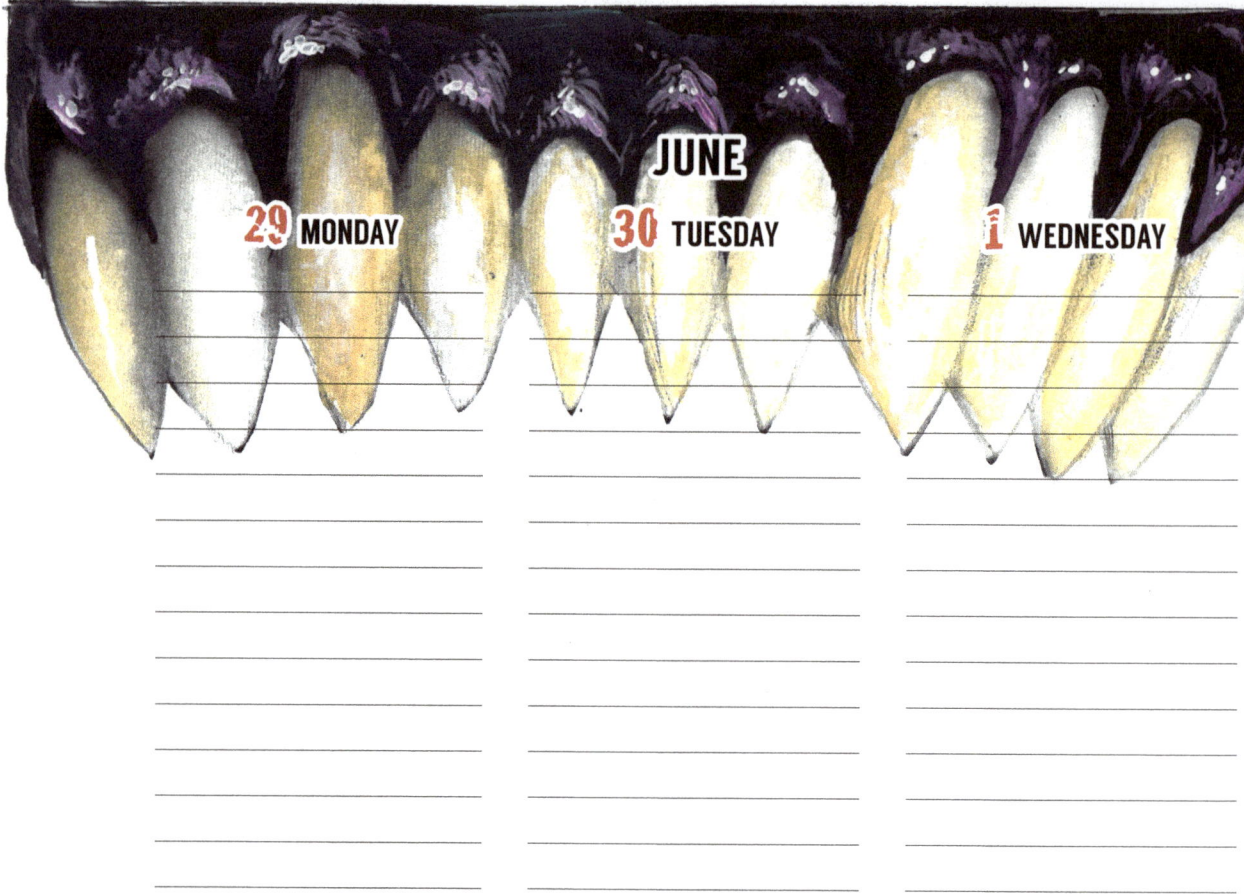

Art by Allen Koszowski

through night two stood up, stretched, sort of smiled. It said to me it had his support, and I think he decided in that reading, yeah, let's do it. The producers had a brainstorm, and they picked up the phone, and they made an overture toward George Romero. He loved the book. He was as nuts for it, as I was. He saw the possibilities of what it could be. I pitched it to the network as a long novel for television, and I said, 'I think it should be eight and ideally, ten hours. We exchanged maybe 5 times in the course of the process. I would do what was needed which was called a Bible in Television terms, which was just a really detailed outline, and I'd send it to George. He'd look at the outline and a week later. I would get a 45-page typed version of mine

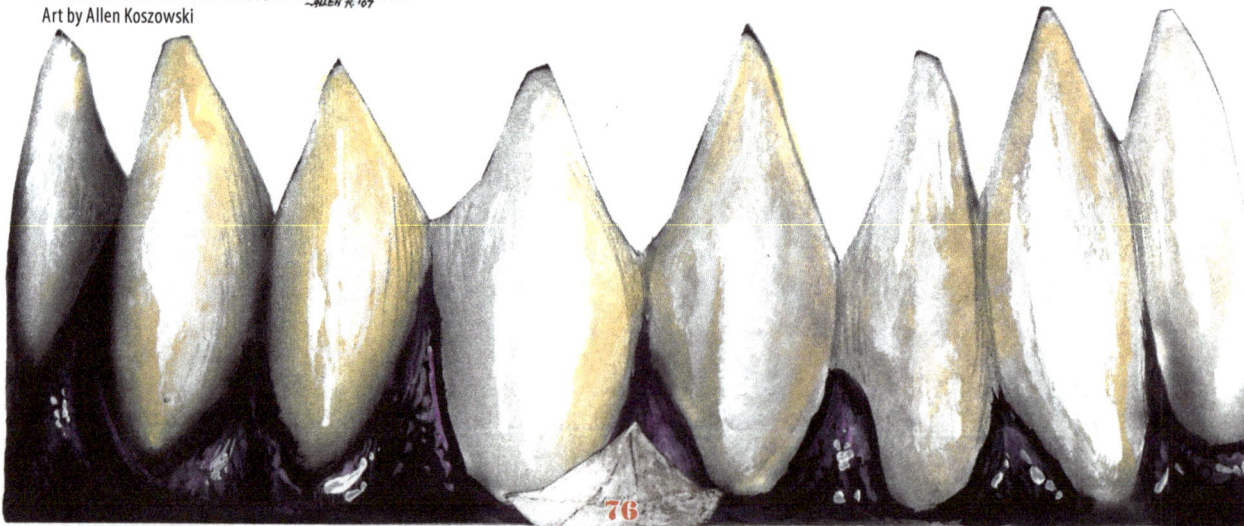

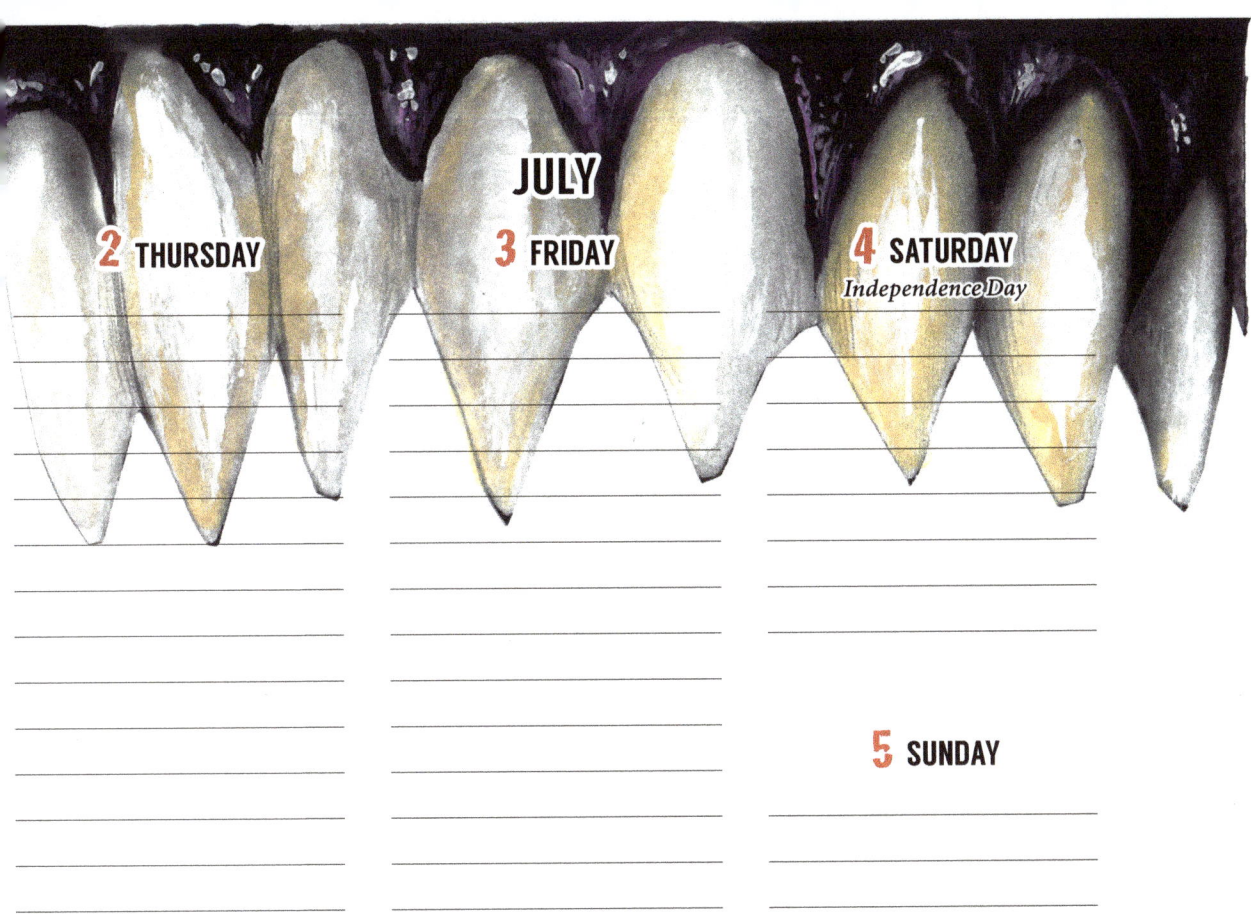

JULY

2 THURSDAY

3 FRIDAY

4 SATURDAY
Independence Day

5 SUNDAY

interspersed with his thoughts. His notes and his suggestions There was never a question that he thought it was going to be a gross out, lots of blood, kind of picture. He understood what television offered was the chance for you to go right up to the line, but his radar was out for what would the network allow? I think the dream of what we had in mind, was absolutely amazing. I think we were just about 20 years early in having it, we would have been *Game of Thrones*. That would have been the way to do this piece of material in its fullest possible way. The network started to get very nervous. Nobody had ever gone where this piece had gone, and they sort of went from it being 8 hours, which became the official running time Bible to maybe it should be 4 at which point George said 'goodbye.' – Lawrence Cohen

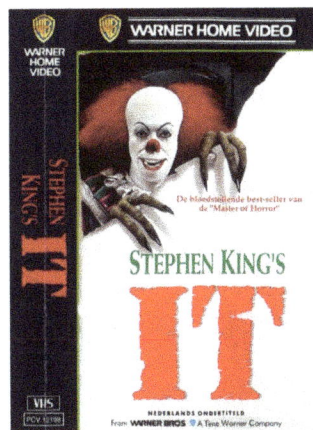

IT, VHS, Dutch 1990

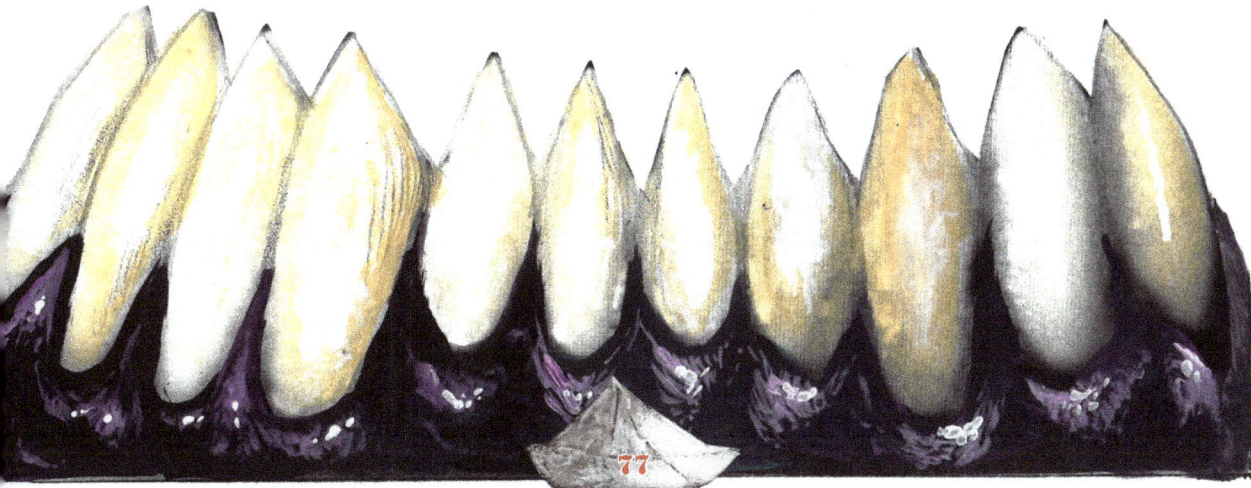

JULY

Charlie Howard

On the evening of July 7, 1984, Charlie Howard had attended a church potluck supper. Later, around 10:30 p.m., he was walking in downtown Bangor, arm-in-arm with his friend Roy Ogden. They were going to Harlow Street to pick up Howard's mail from his post office box. That's when three young men crossed their path. Daniel Ness, 17, Shawn I. Mabry, 16, and James Francis Baines, 15, they had spent the day drinking alcohol, gained illegally thru a friend of legal age to buy for them. That's when they saw Charlie and Roy. Later they told the Bangor police they just wanted to beat up a "faggot" — something they claimed to have done before. As Charlie and Roy were running from them, Charlie tripped and fell. The drunken teenagers started kicking him and then threw him over the bridge railing into the Kenduskeag Stream, 15 feet below. He couldn't swim. He died by drowning, with an acute asthma attack as a contributing factor. In 2014 the *Bangor Daily News* republished a story on the 40th anniversary on Charlie Howard who was murdered in Bangor, Maine, by a group of young men in 1984. Because

Bangor Daily News, Charlie Howard 40th anniversary 2014

78

JULY

9 THURSDAY

10 FRIDAY

11 SATURDAY

12 SUNDAY

he was gay. 1984 was a very different time, not that we should be complacent in today's world, but back then the attitude towards the LGBTQ community could be vicious. Unfortunately, Charlie Howard was at the wrong place, at the wrong time and paid the ultimate price for his lifestyle in the hands of ignorant drunken teenagers.

Stephen King was writing his novel *IT* at the time of Charlie Howard's murder. He was outraged by this senseless murder and it became a significant inspiration for the character of Adrian Mellon in the novel. This scene was included at the beginning of the film *IT Chapter Two*. Much like the scene in *IT*, the character of Adrian Mellon was acted by Xavier Dolan, a Canadian director and actor. Dolan's involvement was notable because of his own identity as a gay man, which added weight to the portrayal of a character who is targeted for his sexuality.

"I think the death of Charlie Howard shocked people in the Bangor area out of their complacency about matters of sexual preference and prejudice. I know it did me. It's easy enough to see what happened as a stupid crime, a kind of felonious accident, fueled by booze; hazing that got out of hand. Probably too easy. In the aftermath of this inoffensive young man's death, the community underwent a period of self-examination that hasn't ended to this day. To me that suggests one good thing came out of Charlie Howard's death, but when I look back on it, I'm still overcome with feelings of sadness and shame. I don't feel responsible, exactly, and I'd never lay that on the community. But it's our town. We live here. Which means we have to live with Charlie, and continue trying to make it right."

— Stephen King, Spring 2014

You can read the complete article at **www.bangordailynews.com/projects/2014/06/charlie/**

JULY

13 MONDAY

14 TUESDAY

15 WEDNESDAY

Pennywise is an American punk rock band from Hermosa Beach, California, formed in 1988. The band took its name from that monster we know so well in Stephen King's horror novel *IT*, known as Pennywise. No, Pennywise did not get permission from Stephen King to use the name. The band used the name as a metaphor rather than an explicit reference. Lead singer Jim Lindberg explained that the monster in *IT* "would turn into whatever scared you the most". He said the band's use of the name represented a "metaphor for the band: here's a band that's loud and scary...but it's bringing you a change". Between their 1991 self-titled debut and 2005's *The Fuse*, Pennywise released an album every two years on Epitaph Records, a label owned by Bad Religion guitarist Brett Gurewitz. To date, the band has released twelve full-length studio albums, one live album, two

This T-shirt is available at **pennywisdom.com**

JULY

16 THURSDAY

17 FRIDAY

18 SATURDAY

19 SUNDAY

EPs and one DVD. Although their first two studio albums were critically acclaimed, Pennywise would not experience worldwide commercial success until the 1995 release of their third studio album, *About Time*, which peaked at number ninety-six on the Billboard 200. Their self-titled first album, *Pennywise*, does feature a song "Pennywise" and these lyrics seem to be the only reference, outside of the band name, that I can find to referencing the character in *IT*:

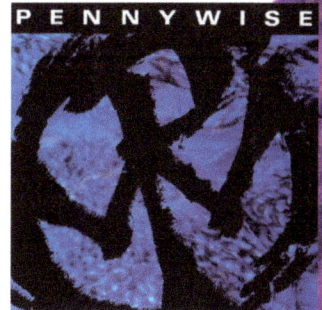

Clear your mind, Hide your fear, Don't look around, Don't turn around Pennywise is here Hold your feelings, Hide your fear, Don't look around, Don't turn around Pennywise is here [Chorus] Evil lurks in his eyes, The clown they call Pennywise, He'll catch you by surprise The clown they call Pennywise He's a monster, He's not human, He's more than just a figment of your imagination, You can't run can't hide, There's no way to escape Pennywise [Chorus repeats] You can visit their website at **pennywisdom.com**

20 MONDAY

21 TUESDAY

22 WEDNESDAY

CHARLES IN CHARGE

The exclusive Limited Edition of Stephen King's, *The Life of Chuck*. Here's a look, probably the only look, we'll get to see of this Mike Flanagan production. Mike Flanagan—writer and director of *The Haunting of Hill House*, *Doctor Sleep*, *Midnight Mass*, and many others—asked Lyra's Books if they would like to create a very limited-edition keepsake for his new film, *The Life of Chuck*. Based on the Stephen King novella, premiered at the 2024 Toronto International Film Festival, September 2024. Mike Flanagan commissioned a special edition of just 30 copies which were privately distributed as gifts to those involved with the film. These were not offered to the public. The book includes Stephen King's original story alongside the script for the film. It also features essays and signatures from Stephen King, Mike Flanagan, Tom Hiddleston, Chiwetel Ejiofor, Karen Gillan and Mark Hamill.

Artist Greg Manchess created three paintings: a tipped-in frontispiece and two additional tipped-in illustrations within the short story. The text design and layout were masterfully handled by Marcelo Anciano of Areté Editions The book also contains numerous black-and-white behind-the-scenes photographs printed directly onto the page, along with 17 tipped-in color images from the movie. The text and black-and-white images were digitally printed on 148gsm Mohawk Superfine Eggshell paper. The books were bound in cream goat leather, foil-blocked with dancing Chucks/Toms across the entire cover in three colors. The page edges were hand-gilded in gold, and the hand-marbled paper was crafted by the amazingly talented Freya Scott of Paperwilds . The Chuck/Tom Hiddleston head on the front of the leather solander box is a cut-out in the board and leather, revealing marbled paper beneath, symbolizing the universes contained within life itself—the multitudes we contain, and, in this case specifically, the multitudes Chuck contains.

JULY

23 THURSDAY

24 FRIDAY

25 SATURDAY

26 SUNDAY

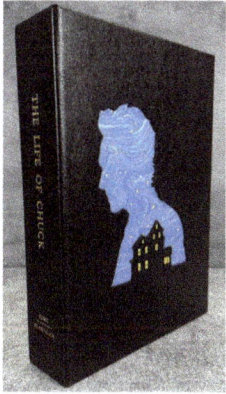

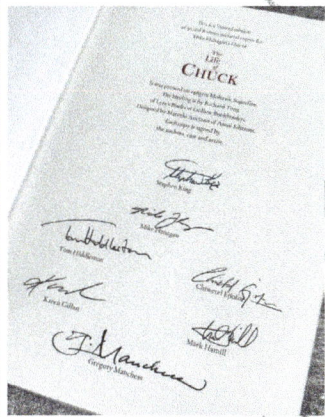

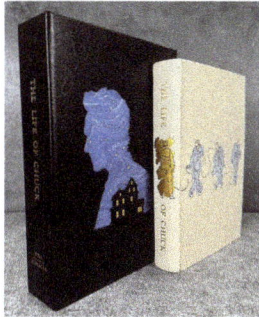

*Please note — there were never any copies of this book for sale and this is not an edition published by Lyra's Books or Arete Editions. This was a private commission and published under the name of Mike Flanagan's own Multitude Press.

The Life of Chuck limited edition, 30 copies for private distribution, Multitude Press 2024

27 MONDAY

28 TUESDAY

29 WEDNESDAY

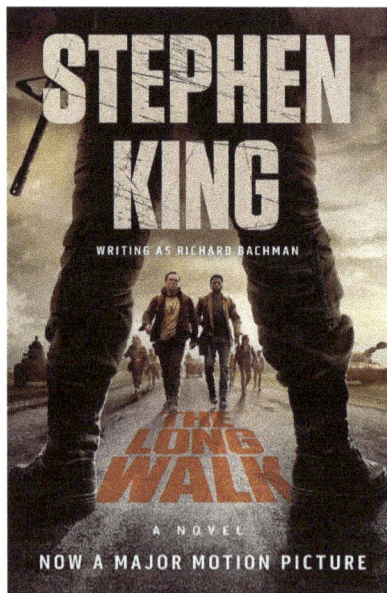

The Long Walk, Movie Cover Edition, Scribner 2025

THE MAJOR MEETS KIMMEL

Mark Hamill was featured as a guest on Jimmy Kimmel Live September 3rd, 2025 to promote the Stephen King film, *The Long Walk*. Here's a moment where Jimmy Kimmel talks about the Stephen King connection with Mark Hamill.

JK: "Did Stephen King have any involvement in the film itself?"

MH: "Well, it's funny, when I went to the Toronto Film Festival, they said, 'oh, you're going to sit right next to Stephen King.' That's when I knew I was a good actor because I went out and said 'how do you do, nice to meet you'. . . but inside I'm going *oh my God, it's Stephen King!*"

JK: "Oh, he's one of your guys, too."

MH: "Oh, I love that man. When he looked up at me (Mark Hamill is recreating Stephen King pointing the finger at him) and said 'the Major!'"

JULY

30 THURSDAY

_____
_____
_____
_____
_____
_____
_____
_____
_____
_____
_____
_____
_____
_____
_____

31 FRIDAY

_____
_____
_____
_____
_____
_____
_____
_____
_____
_____
_____
_____

1 SATURDAY

_____
_____
_____
_____
_____
_____
_____
_____

2 SUNDAY

_____
_____

JK: "Oh, that's your character!"

MH: "That's my character. We haven't filmed it yet. I said, 'how does he know?' But afterwards I asked the people from Lionsgate, 'how did he know?' They said, 'oh, after a few bad early experiences, he has casting control, director control, script control, over everything. So, he knew that I'd been cast, and I thought that was, yeah…'"

JK: "That's a nice compliment to get for sure."

JK: "Yeah, this had a screening where you had the… this is really strange, you had the audience on treadmills, and they had to walk At 3 miles or above for the whole film, or else what happened?"

MH: "You gotta love an audience, that's committed. Because I have to tell you the first thing I was asking about I said, 'wait a minute, the long walk, how much walking do I do in this film?' None, I'm in a Jeep, the whole time and loving it. But I mean, I'm watching videos of these people on the Treadmill. The treadmills are going the same speed that the guys are supposed to walk in the movie. And I thought, what dedication and if you fail, they don't shoot you in the head, but they escort you out of the screenings."

3 MONDAY

4 TUESDAY

5 WEDNESDAY

TOMMY'S TAKE ON *IT*

AN - During your career, you've tackled some pretty big franchises. However, one of the biggest projects you took on was the Stephen King epic novel, *IT*. How did this project come about, and how hard was it to bring a 1000+ page classic horror novel to the television screen over a two-night, 2-hour episode each of those nights?

TLW - *IT* came to me in the conventional way: Certain interested parties contacted my agent about the directing gig, I went to a meeting, must've said the right things, and got hired right away. By the time I came on board, the project had been around for a while, a lot of the budget had been spent coming up with a viable script, and a more ambitious mini-series of several nights had been gradually whittled down to two. I don't know for certain, but I suspect that what may have gotten me the gig was my reputation for wringing decent results out of shoestring budgets and impossible schedules. The biggest challenges were, as you suggest, in the script. *IT* is a marvelous novel. It takes its time, and goes many, many places as it tells its tale of a group of children who bond with each other and bolster themselves against unspeakable evil, both as kids,

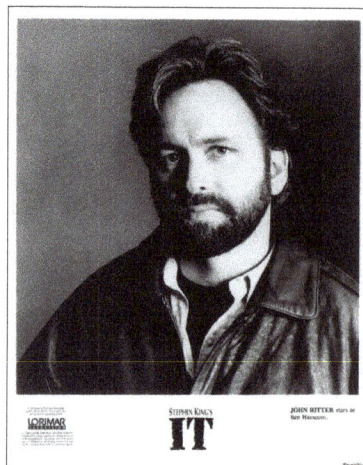

John Ritter, *IT* press photo, ABC 1990

AUGUST

6 THURSDAY

7 FRIDAY

8 SATURDAY

9 SUNDAY

and then again as adults. Larry Cohen's script for Night One is a masterpiece, the only time I've ever seen TV's seven-act movie structure used effectively as a dramatic tool. Seven-act TV movie structure is purely in service of commerce, not art or drama; it's a way of cramming as many commercials into the program as is humanly possible, without completely losing the thread of the story. Fortunately for us, and thanks to Larry's skill, the seven acts proved ideal for introducing the seven key characters, one by one, as their adult lives are interrupted by terrifying news calling them back to their collective childhoods: *IT* has returned. That was Night 1. As good as that script was, the Night 2 script left a lot to be desired. Suffice it to say that after quite a bit of rewriting, I wound up telling the story as best as I could, given the time limitations, both in pre-production, and in the predetermined length of the show. In the end, one could say the *IT* miniseries was a sort of Reader's Digest condensed version of the novel. As to the epic, universal conflict featured in the climax of the book, the cosmic turtle and all that — well, there are just some things a novel can do that a movie cannot.

— Tommy Lee Wallace, Director of *IT* (1990).
Interview by Anthony Northrup

THE STEPHEN KING CATALOG

2024 ANNUAL

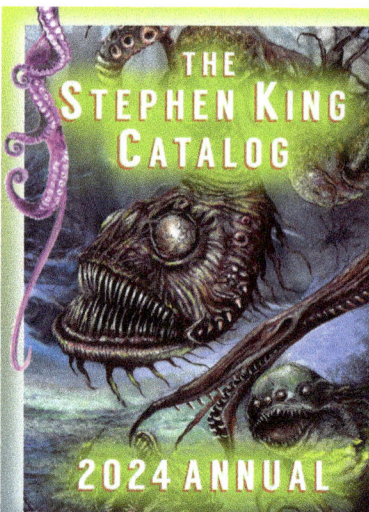

2024 STEPHEN KING ANNUAL: THE MIST

The Stephen King Annual, with articles, interviews, and a 52-week Calendar of Facts and Triva! Full-color! **Over 230 Pages our largest edition yet!** *The Mist*, 40 years in print, 15 years on film.

Dave Hinchberger's Introduction **The Storm is Coming. Dave's Entering... The Mist** 5,000-words of three-days on the set, including a visit with Greg Nicotero (now of *The Walking Dead* fame). Also **The Making of Stephen King's The Mist Angelsoft Game.**

▶ **Glenn Chadbourne's** original wrap-around cover and interior artwork throughout.

▶ **Bev Vincent's The Mist: Interviews – On the Set of** *The Mist.* Extensive interviews with actors Marcia Gay Harden, Toby Jones, and Thomas Jane. Also, his annual write-up of Everything King – Current and Upcoming Releases.

▶ **Un-Filmed Scene From** *The Mist* storyboard art with *Mist* artist **Pete Von Sholly.**

▶ **Stephen Bissette** is an artist and film enthusiast explores in-depth examination of *The Mist* film and story here with his unique critique.

▶ **Kevin Quigley** on **"The Mist"** 3-D audio drama. The author delves into the history of this ground-breaking audio from the 1980's. Kevin also gives us **Mist Opportunities: The Long Story of a Short Novel.**

▶ **Constantine Nasr's Misty Memories** official account of working on *The Mist* film as the official videographer for director Frank Darabont, with stories and photos.

▶ **Tyson Blue's** look at the rare column Stephen **King's Garbage Truck** is examined in detail with fascinating results that later appear in King's fiction.

▶ **Stephen Spignesi** brings us the latest uncollected Stephen King writings with **The New Lost Work of Stephen King.**

▶ **Andrew Rausch** interviews *The Mist* film storyboard artist, **Pete Von Sholly: The Man of Many Hats.**

▶ **Pete Von Sholly** shares his previously unpublished story in comic book form, "The Missed," based on his working on *The Mist* film. Premiering here in *The Mist* edition!

▶ **L.L. Soares** *The Mist*, book to movie screen / TV screen, every version analyzed.

▶ **Ariel Bosi** reviews *Holly* by Stephen King.

▶ **Noah Mitchel & Diana Petroff** begin their first column of unique Stephen King collectibles titled **"Extreme King."** Featuring *Dark Forces*, first appearance of *The Mist* story.

▶ **Anthony Northrup's** annual Dollar Baby Review will examine a current Stephen King Dollar Baby film. He highlights **"The Monkey"** 2023 film with a review and interview.

▶ **Dave Hinchberger's** annual calendar entry features fifty-two weeks of trivia and facts around each Annual's theme. Wait until you see what he pulls out of *The Mist*!

Order at **StephenKingCatalog.com** Additional details and FREE Exclusive Extras! PLUS! A limited edition with an Exclusive cover, Signed! Trade edition is also at Amazon.com, BN.com, and other retailers.
Price: 49.95 ISBN: 978-1-62330-706-6 In Stock!

Published by
Overlook Connection Press

The Mist Limited Edition Lithograph Only 500 Signed Copies
17" x 11" Signed / Numbered by artist **Glenn Chadbourne**

Skeleton Crew: Unpublished Stephen King Anniversary Cover Lithograph Only 500 Signed Copies 17" x 11" Signed / Numbered by artist **Pete Von Sholly**

Search for LITHOGRAPH at **StephenKingCatalog.com**

OVERLOOK CONNECTION PRESS

2023 Overlook Connection Press. Sent Rolled.

Artwork © 2023 Glenn Chadbourne

Artwork © 2023 Pete Von Sholly

AUGUST

10 MONDAY | **11** TUESDAY | **12** WEDNESDAY

PRINT *IT*

IT, 9/50 by Robert Giusti Limited Edition Print. Hand Numbered Limited Edition Screen Print Variant (24" X 36"). This limited edition silkscreen print was created by the original hardcover artist, Robert Giusti, based off the original 1986 Viking hardcover release of Stephen King's classic horror novel *IT*. This same artwork was later used as the cover for one of the VHS releases of the original *IT* miniseries. These high-quality, limited edition prints, and exclusive giclée and silkscreen offerings are part pop culture and part fine art, illustrating unique reimagining's of cult media created by some of the most renowned commercial and

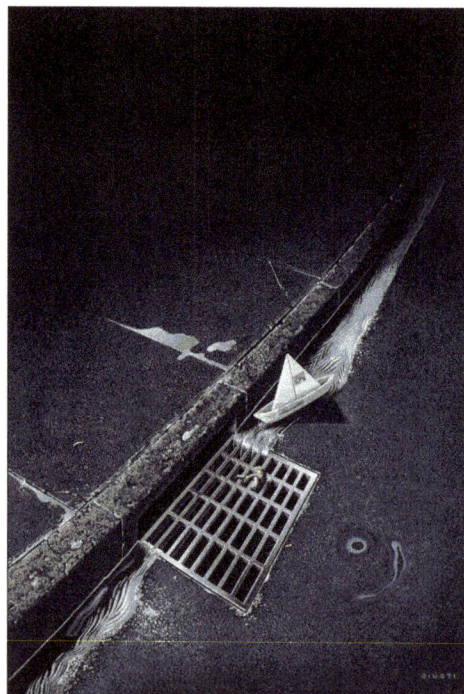

1 of 50 Alternate *IT* posters by Robert Giusti. Lady Lazarus 2017

AUGUST

13 THURSDAY

14 FRIDAY

15 SATURDAY

16 SUNDAY

comic art illustrators of the day. Known for selling out of stock within mere minutes when offered online by the individual artist, these prints also make their special debuts at collaborating galleries and such famed events like the San Diego and New York Comic Cons. Ultimately, these highly sought-after prints have become coveted items among movie fans and play a greater part in the future of the collecting hobby. This limited run poster of *IT* was released by Lady Lazarus in 2017, and is hand numbered. The poster was created in two different styles, this being the regular edition. The poster has never been used or displayed. Only the most minimal signs of handling to the exterior of the poster due to storage are acceptable. It was auctioned off at Heritage Auctions in September 2023 for $71.00.

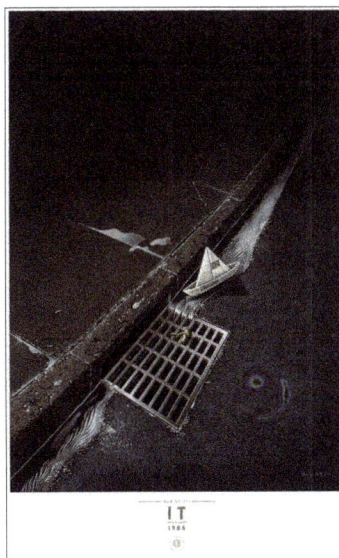

Suntup Covers Collection. *IT*, signed by artist Robert Giusti, 2017. Available at Suntup Press

AUGUST

17 MONDAY   **18** TUESDAY   **19** WEDNESDAY

THE LOOK OF *IT*

An interview with Bart Mixon

Houston, Texas-born Bart Mixon began working as a special make-up effects artist in the early 1980s. He has worked on more than 150 films, including such well-known and highly-regarded films as *RoboCop*, *Hellboy*, *Iron Man*, *Star Trek*, *Guardians of the Galaxy*, and *Avengers: Infinity War*, just to name a few. More specific to our purposes, Mixon worked his magic on the 1990 TV mini-series *IT*, for which he crafted the look of Tim Curry's iconic Pennywise character. Although that's what he's primarily known for in terms of *IT*, Mixon was the Make-up Effects Supervisor and oversaw all aspects of creature effects for the series.

Were you a Stephen King fan before working on *IT*? I wasn't a huge fan. I had read *Pet Sematary* and loved it. And I read *Night Shift*, with "Jerusalem's Lot" and some of the others. My twin brother, Bret, who also worked on the visual effects for *IT*—he did the animation for the head-lights coming out of Pennywise's head—was a huge King fan. So, he told me about *IT* while he was reading it, so I was certainly aware of it. I guess I'm just not as much of a reader as he was, but I enjoyed *Night Shift* and *Pet Sematary*.

Did you meet Stephen King while you were working on *IT*? Unfortunately, no. As far as I know, King never came by the set. I think they invited him. I assume he was too busy. I prepped the show in Burbank. We shot in Vancouver over eight weeks. I flew back and forth every week, once or twice a week. Because I was not only in charge of Pennywise, but all the other manifestations of *IT*.

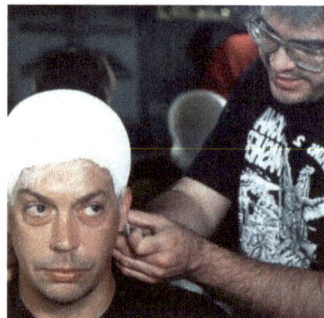

Tim Curry makeup photos by Bart Mixon, 1990

92

23 SUNDAY

So, I had to go back and forth to make sure my crew was continuing work. So, King visited the set, it wasn't while I was there. But as I understand it, he never came by the set.

Were there earlier concepts of what Pennywise was going to look like? Were there earlier versions of Pennywise, either in sketches or models?
Everything, conceptually, was generated by me working in tandem with Tommy (director). Before they cast [Tim Curry], I did try a little bit of sketching, just to get some ideas. But make-ups like this are very actor-driven, and it needs to be designed over the actor. So, whatever I tried to do pre-Tim Curry was pretty futile. Once Tim was cast and I got a head shot, I started with a sketch of his head—basically a

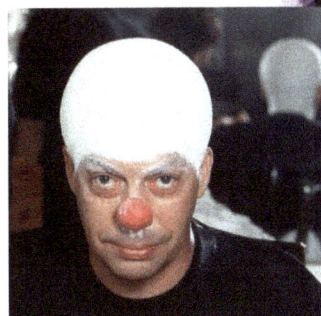

Tim Curry makeup photos by Bart Mixon, 1990

tracing—and then I just started drawing different clown concepts over that. Tommy was already in Vancouver, so I would fax those up to him and get his feedback. Then I would make modifications based on that. I looked at those drawings recently. I think I had maybe five or six different basic head shapes. Some were very light on prosthetics. I think some had virtually no prosthetics. Some were much heavier, you know, like full face coverage. We just went back and forth. Tommy basically picked three that he liked. Then I did what is called a clay sketch, where I took three copies of Tim Curry's life mask and three different quick sculptures of the different concepts that Tommy liked. I did a quick paint job and threw a quick wig on him and took photos of that, and then I sent those to Tommy. Then he selected the one from those three that he liked best, that we then developed into an actual prosthetic make-up, which entailed me re-sculpting it and breaking it down to the various components that it would be applied.

What was Tim Curry like to work with? I'm guessing you had to work pretty closely with him to apply the make-up each day? I had a Canadian assistant named Joanne Smith, so the two of us applied it on a daily basis. Tim was great. He was certainly no stranger to prosthetics at that point, having been Darkness in *Legend*, which is why I think he wanted as little

AUGUST

24 MONDAY

25 TUESDAY

26 WEDNESDAY

prosthetic as he could get away with on this show. He was 100 percent pro. He was very nice. That might have been about the first time I was maybe star-struck working with an actor. I was certainly familiar with him from *Rocky Horror Picture Show* and *Legend* and a few other things, so it was the first time I felt a little intimidated, even though I'd worked with Shelly Winters and a few people like that prior. But Tim was great. He was a very good collaborator. When we did our make-up tests, he had some ideas in mind for the paint schemes, so our first test reflected those. The second test was closer to what Tommy had approved in my design stage. Then we ended up somewhere in the middle.

People don't tend to talk as much about the other pieces that you did on that film, because Pennywise gets all the attention. Let's talk about some of the other pieces. Let's talk about the werewolf. That was actually a buddy of mine, Norman Cabrera. It's like that old saying, you're only as good as your crew. So, I knew from the start, with all the traveling back and forth to Canada, that I would only have time to actually sculpt the Pennywise makeup. But I would be taking everything on set. I also knew, scheduling-wise, that the werewolf and Pennywise were going to work on the same day, and also, just from reading the script, that the werewolf didn't play in it a lot. We decided to do him as an over-the-head mask as opposed to a prosthetic makeup.

Tim Curry makeup photos by Bart Mixon, 1990

94

AUGUST

27 THURSDAY

28 FRIDAY

29 SATURDAY

30 SUNDAY

Tim Curry makeup photos by Bart Mixon, 1990

So, there was basically a spandex hood that covered his neck that had the hair tied in it. Then we had a mask that ended at his jawline at the base of his skull that went over that. So, it was a very quick on and off application. Then he had the werewolf gloves.

What are your thoughts on *IT*'s legacy and continued popularity, all of these years later?
I don't know if surprised is the right word, but. . . I'm certainly grateful. I was talking with [legendary make-up artist] Rick Baker about stuff like this once and I said, "Well, it's nice to have one [iconic character]." You know, Rick's got a career filled with iconic characters, but Pennywise was something that was my design, my sculpture, my application, so it was kind of my baby from start to finish. It's nice to have one that people remember. I'm certainly grateful that people remember it. I think it took a little while for it to achieve the cult status that it has now. I think there were some rights issues back in the late '90s and early 2000's that prevented, say, Mcfarlane Toys from making action figures and stuff from it. Thankfully, Warner Bros. got everything squared away in time for their remake in 2017, which I think has rekindled the interest in my version (and the Tim Curry version). — Interview by Andrew J. Rausch

Read more of the complete Bart Mixon interview in the
2026 Stephen King Annual: IT 40th Anniversary.

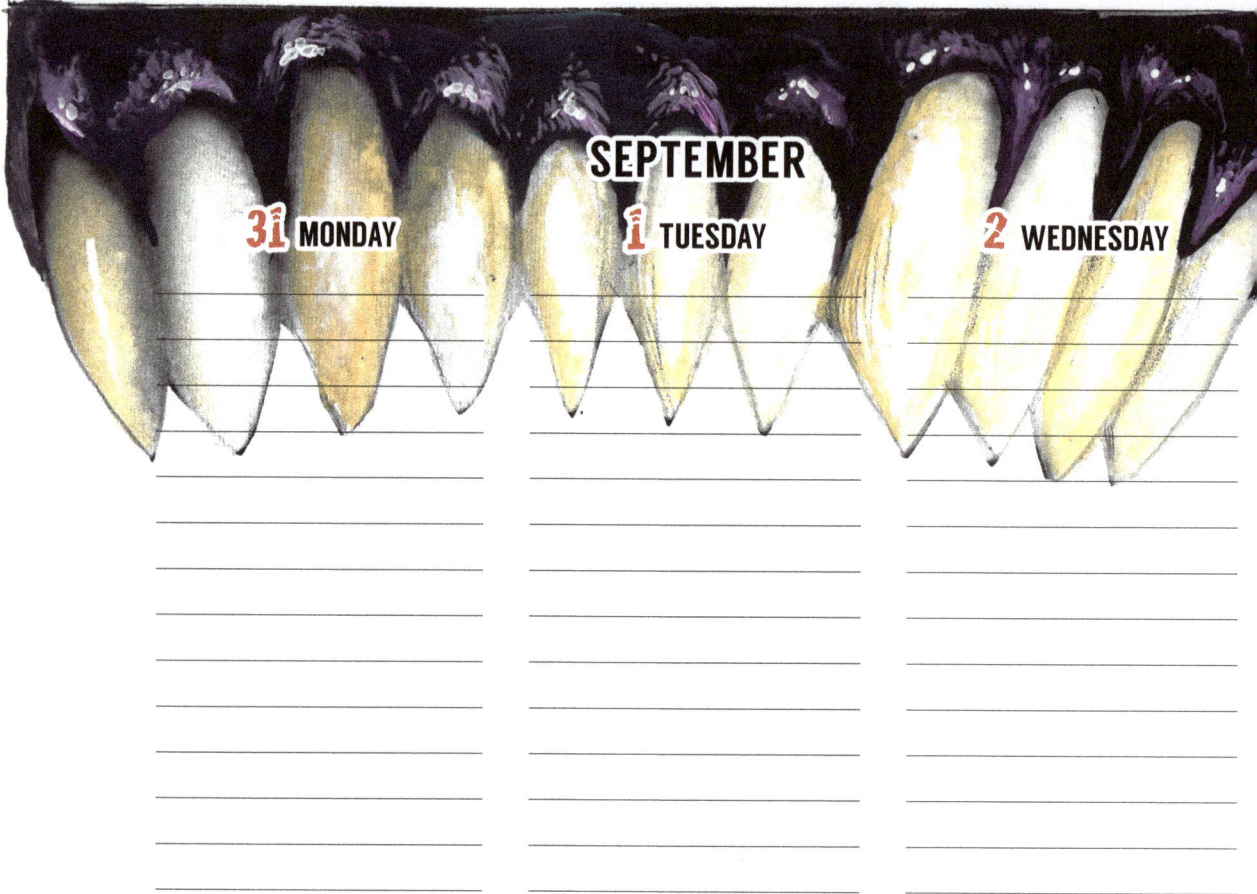

SEPTEMBER

31 MONDAY	1 TUESDAY	2 WEDNESDAY

¡7 SIGNATURES!

IT CHAPTER TWO Signed Advance Movie Poster This signed *IT Chapter Two* (2019) one-sheet (27" x 40") is signed by 17 of the cast and crew. This signed theatrical poster was sold at auction for $1,134 on September 13th, 2024. Can you name all the signatures shown here? Get out your magnifying glass some of these are tricky.

Answers:

Signed by Bill Skarsgård, Jessica Chastain, James McAvoy, Bill Hader, Isaiah Mustafa, Jay Ryan, James Ransone, Andy Bean, Jaeden Martell, Wyatt Oleff, Jack Dylan Grazer, Finn Wolfhard, Sophia Lillis, Chosen Jacobs, Jeremy Ray Taylor. Also signed by producer Barbara Muschietti and director Andy Muschietti.

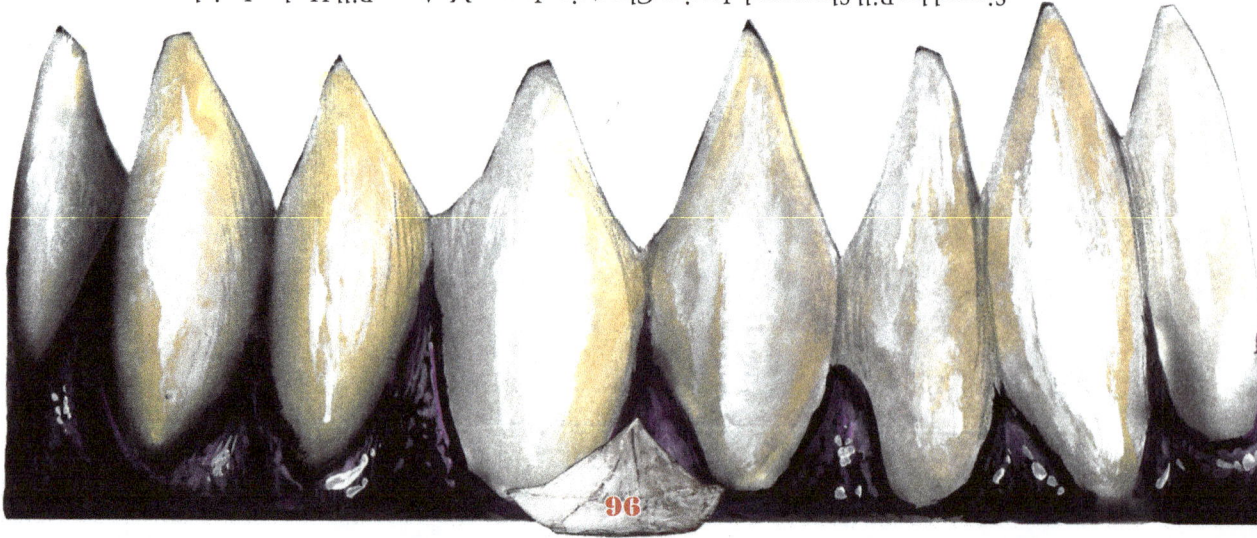

SEPTEMBER

3 THURSDAY

4 FRIDAY

5 SATURDAY

6 SUNDAY

IT Chapter Two advance theater poster, Warner Bros. 2019

7 MONDAY	**8** TUESDAY	**9** WEDNESDAY
Labor Day		

DISPLAY *IT*

The *IT* Art Gallery – August 31 – September 3rd, 2017 Warner Bros. Pictures and Director Andy Muschietti adapted the brilliant, brutal, gory, disturbing novel by author Stephen King, bringing *IT*, to the big screen. This R-rated horror film stars: Bill Skarsgard, Jaeden Lieberher, Jeremy Ray Raylor, Sophia Lillis, Finn Wolfhard, Wyatt Oleff, Chosen Jacobs, Jack Dylan Grazer, Nicholas Hamilton, and Jackson Robert Scott and hit theaters on September 6th, 2017.

Artists officially collaborated with Warner Bros. Pictures to help promote the theatrical release by creating 5 images along with an animated process video that were shown exclusively on social media by AMC Theaters, Fandango, iHorror and ComingSoon.net. These posters were on display at Gallery 1988 in Los Angeles. The exhibit, "The *IT* Art Gallery" opened from August 31 – September 3rd in 2017. If you like your nightmares filled with disturbing, shape-shifting clowns…..then this was the spot to be. They recommended that we should "book an appointment with your therapist after you go to the exhibit." Maybe *IT*'s a good thing we couldn't make it!

THE IT ART GALLERY
AT GALLERY1988
8/31/17 - 9/3/17
7308 MELROSE AVENUE
LOS ANGELES, CA 90046
11AM – 6PM
#ITMovie
NEW LINE CINEMA

Warner Bros.
Promo poster gallery, 2017

SEPTEMBER

10 THURSDAY

11 FRIDAY

12 SATURDAY
Rosh Hashanah

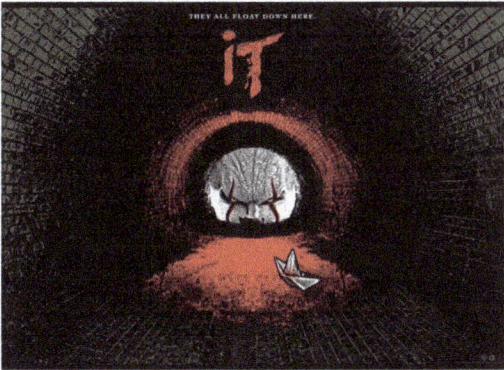

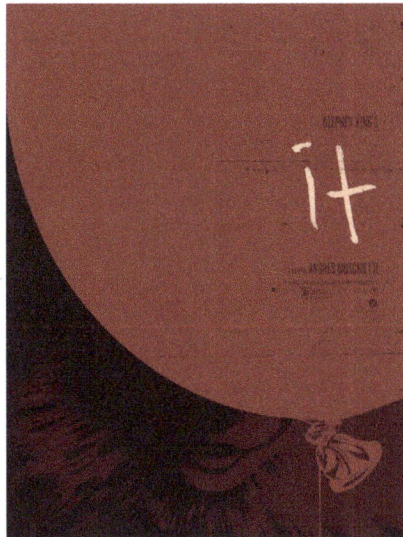

13 SUNDAY
Rosh Hashanah

Warner Bros. Promo poster gallery, 2017

SEPTEMBER

14 MONDAY

15 TUESDAY

16 WEDNESDAY

RARE *IT* ARTWORK

Hand-Drawn Jeremy Pailler Giveaway Poster Concept Artwork a Poster of the final art. Concept artwork hand-drawn by illustrator Jeremy Pailler for a special giveaway poster distributed by Warner Bros. to Odeon Cinemas for promotional screenings of Andy Muschietti's *IT.* This concept 8.5" x 11.5" (21.75 cm x 29.25 cm) artwork depicting Pennywise (Bill Skarsgard) with the Losers Club in his hand is rendered in graphite on paper and signed "J. Pailler IT 2017." The artwork is considered rare as a different final design was ultimately used for the poster as shown here in color. Poster is printed in full color with the Warner Bros copyright at bottom. Dimensions: (largest) 11.5" x 16.5" (29.25 cm x 42 cm). This artwork sold in July, 2025, for a winning bid of $378.

IT color poster art by Jeremy Pailler for WB 2017

SEPTEMBER

17 THURSDAY   **18** FRIDAY   **19** SATURDAY

20 SUNDAY

IT sketch poster art by Jeremy Pailler for WB 2017

21 MONDAY
Yom Kippur

22 TUESDAY

23 WEDNESDAY

"It's amazing to me all these years later, people are still coming up and talking about it, that it has this lasting effect and impact."

– Richard Thomas

Actor Richard Thomas on the effect the series of *IT* has had on fans.
He plays Bill Denbrough as an adult, *IT* 1990 ABC series.

SEPTEMBER

24 THURSDAY

25 FRIDAY

26 SATURDAY

27 SUNDAY

IT, Losers' Club
adult photo,
Warner Bros. 1990

Glenn
Chadbourne

Harry Anderson, Richard Thomas, Dennis Christopher, Annette O'Toole and John Ritter star as childhood friends who reunite to confront an evil entity that haunted them 30 years ago and has returned to scare and kill again, on the ABC Novel for Television, **STEPHEN KING'S "IT,"** airing **SUNDAY, NOV. 18** and **TUESDAY, NOV. 20** (9:00-11:00 p.m., ET, both days), on the ABC Television Network.   Photo credit: Craig Sjodin/ABC.   JSP 10/30/90   27580A-8-6

ABC Photography Department 77 West 66 Street, New York, New York 10023 (212) 456-7777
© 1990 COPYRIGHT CAPITAL CITIES/ABC, INC. For editorial use only. All rights reserved.

SEPTEMBER

28 MONDAY

_____
_____
_____
_____
_____
_____
_____
_____
_____
_____
_____

29 TUESDAY

_____
_____
_____
_____
_____
_____
_____
_____
_____
_____
_____

30 WEDNESDAY

_____
_____
_____
_____
_____
_____
_____
_____
_____
_____
_____

TWO AUTHORS WHO ARE "IT"

Stephen King pays tribute to many authors he read, and authors he considered his mentors and peers within the novel of _IT_. I'm highlighting two authors in particular, Richard Matheson who King grew up reading and watching on the screen, and Dennis Etchison who he worked with.

Dennis Etchison, a horror novelist and editor of horror anthologies, which included Stephen King stories "The Mist" and "Gramma" in _Metahorror_ (1992), and "The Woman in the Room" in _The Complete Masters of Darkness_ (1991). He also wrote the script for the 1984, ZBS Media production of a 90-minute radio version of Stephen King's "The Mist". One of the books mentioned in Stephen King's _Danse Macabre_ is _The Dark Country_ by Dennis Etchison. In _IT_ King pays tribute to one of the horror stories he discovered in one of those men's magazines. He wrote: "One of them, by a man named Dennis Etchison, is actually quite good." In reality this was true as his first story, "Escapades" was sold to a men's magazine when he was still in high-school. King and Etchison had quite a history together at one time.

Dennis Etchison photo by Kris Etchison

OCTOBER

1 THURSDAY

_____
_____
_____
_____
_____
_____
_____
_____
_____
_____
_____
_____
_____

2 FRIDAY

_____
_____
_____
_____
_____
_____
_____
_____
_____
_____
_____
_____
_____

3 SATURDAY

_____
_____
_____
_____
_____
_____
_____

4 SUNDAY

_____
_____
_____
_____

Richard Matheson was a force in Stephen King's life that he's mentioned throughout his writing life. When Matheson passed in 2013 he wrote a piece about the man and his work (you can see in the entirety at StephenKing.Com). He notes that *The Incredible Shrinking Man* and all the wonderful *Twilight Zone* scripts and stories, Matheson fired the imaginations of three generations of writers. Without his *I Am Legend*, there would have been no *Night of the Living Dead*; without *Night of the Living Dead*, there would have been no *Walking Dead*, *28 Days Later*, or *World War Z*. That's a spread of fiction and creation that millions have accessed through the decades. King also notes that "Matheson wrote the script for Steven Spielberg's extraordinary film, *Duel*, and created one of the most brain-freezingly frightening haunted house novels of the 20th century in *Hell House*." King said he created "American scenes I knew and could relate to... I want to do that," I thought. "I must do that." I invite you to pick up the *Nightmares at 20,000 Feet* collection of short fiction to begin on Richard Matheson's work. You'll have the time of your life.

The Richard Matheson Companion,
Gauntlet 2008

OCTOBER

5 MONDAY   **6** TUESDAY   **7** WEDNESDAY

WHO WROTE WHAT?

Stephen King pays tribute to many authors he read, and authors he considered his mentors and peers he pays homage to within the novel of *IT*. Here are just a few mentioned. Can you match up the author with the title of one of their books?

(1.) Richard Matheson

(2.) Ray Bradbury

(3.) H.P. Lovecraft

(4.) George Orwell

(5.) Edgar Allen Poe

(6.) John Updike

(7.) Henry James

(8.) Henry Gregor Felsen

(9.) George Langlahan

(10.) Jack London

(11.) Margaret Mitchell

(12.) H.G. Wells

(13.) Walt Whitman

"May be the scariest haunted house novel ever written."
—STEPHEN KING

"One of the absolute best contemporary horror novels...one of my favorites."
—PETER STRAUB

HELL HOUSE

RICHARD MATHESON

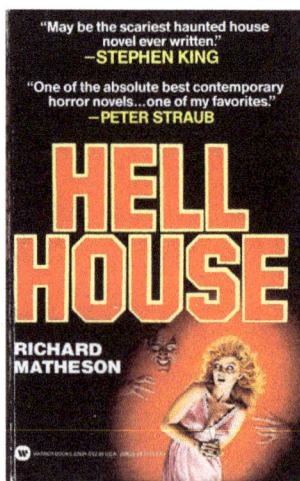

Hell House, Warner Books 1985

The Witches of Eastwick

The Fly

I Am Legend

The Tell-Tale Heart

Something Wicked This Way Comes

The Altar of the Dead

Gone with the Wind

The Dunwich Horror

The War of the Worlds

1984

Leaves of Grass

Hot Rod

The Call of the Wild

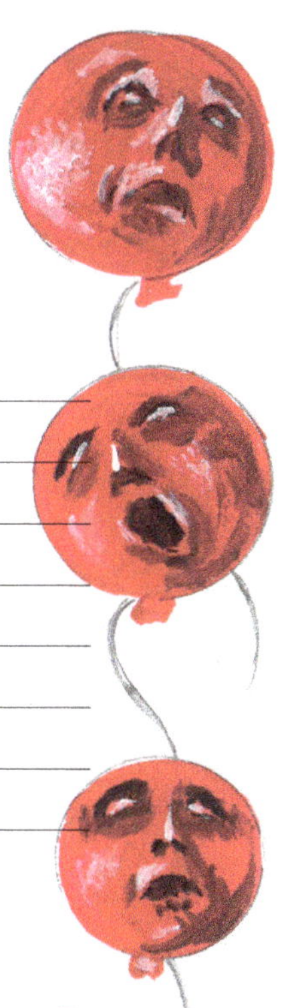

The Halloween Tree
New York: Alfred A. Knopf, 1972

Illustrated by Joseph Mugnaini

THE HALLOWEEN TREE

RAY BRADBURY

Answers:

The Witches of Eastwick (6.)
Author who wrote *The Fly*.
His name is actually spelled
George Langelaan (9.) *I Am
Legend* (1.) *The Tell-Tale Heart*
(5.) *Something Wicked This
Way Comes* (2.) *The Altar
of the Dead* (7.) *Gone with
the Wind* (11.) *The Dunwich
Horror* (3.) *The War of the
Worlds* (12.) *1984* (4.) *Leaves
of Grass*, collection of poems,
published in 1855 (13.) *Hot Rod*
which Ben Hanscom library
borrowed in June 1958. (8.)
The Call of the Wild (10.)

SUNDAY 11

SATURDAY 10

FRIDAY 9

THURSDAY 8

OCTOBER

OCTOBER

THE "HUMAN ELEMENT" OF *IT*

Stephen King gave an interview when he was in Port Hope to film his cameo in *IT Chapter Two* as the Shopkeeper. Stephen King discusses what he thought of *IT* possibly being a hit, the kids, Andy Muschietti's work directing the *IT* films, and reexperiencing his films.

Stephen King: "I saw a rough cut of *IT* in Florida when it was still very much a working cut and not all the effects had finished and it hadn't been color comped. I knew from the first couple of scenes where Georgie is running down the street and chasing his boat, that it was going to be... First of all, I knew that it was good, that it had been made by somebody who understood the material and was going to be really working hard to make a scary picture. And, that he was going to keep on, keep hold of the human element. You see that in the first scenes where Bill and Georgie are together and he's making the boat and Bill can't come out because he's sick. And I said, 'this has a chance to be really good.' And, of course, waiting, what I understood, I think then, that a lot of people maybe had overlooked, was that there was

THE NO. 1 BESTSELLER
STEPHEN KING

NOW A MAJOR
MOTION PICTURE

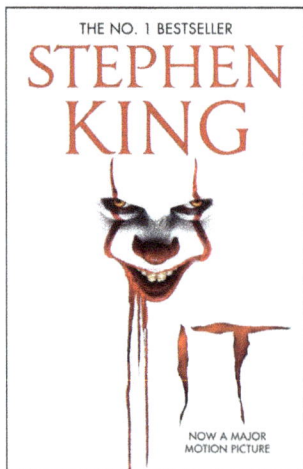

Stephen King, *IT*, Hodder Paperback, 2017

OCTOBER

15 THURSDAY

16 FRIDAY

17 SATURDAY

_____
_____
_____
_____
_____
_____
_____
_____
_____
_____
_____
_____
_____

18 SUNDAY

_____

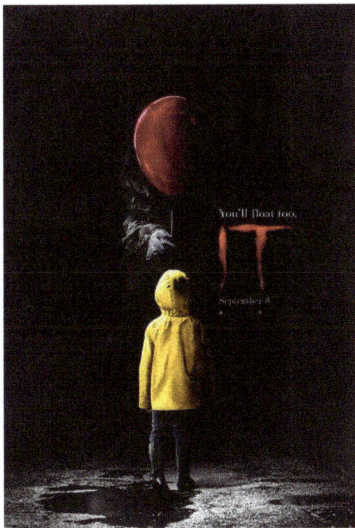

IT (Chapter One) movie poster, Warner Bros. 2017

a whole generation of kids, one generation below mine, who had the pants scared off them by the miniseries where Tim Curry played Pennywise the Clown. I knew that a lot of those people were going to come back to see what we'd done with it. I remember when I was working on the novel, *IT,* and I was living in Bangor which was the basis for Derry, I walked up the street one day and there was this little kid sitting in the dust at the side of the road drawing and talking to herself about imaginary people and what they were doing in her drawings. And I was thinking, if an adult was sitting in the dirt like that and talking to himself, they'd take them away to the nearest mental institution because it would be obvious that they had problems. But, we understand that kids have a wider perspective. Their imaginations are unfettered and as we grow older, it becomes tougher and tougher to hold on to that imagination. So, what I really wanted to do with *IT,* was to bring these people back as adults and they were the only ones who by having this experience when they were kids, had a chance to recapture the imaginative capacity that they had as children. So, that's a fascinating thing.

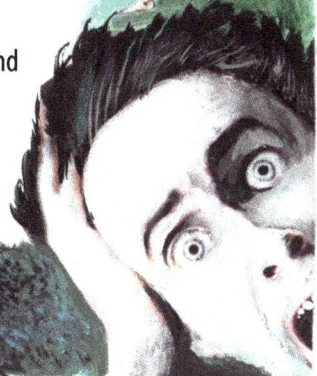

OCTOBER

19 MONDAY   **20** TUESDAY   **21** WEDNESDAY

And, I think that audiences are going to be wowed to see what Andy has done. The thing about this story was there are a lot of romantic ideas about kids and I was able to debunk some of them. And, we see them in *IT*, (part one). They're kids but they have their own inner lives and they have their own rough edges. And, I don't ever have to come out and say the child is father to the man. Or, the child is father to the woman. And, I don't have to spout a lot of new age bullshit about the inner child but those things are all part of the story. I think that's part of the reason that people related to it the way that they did. You know, there are people who went and saw that movie three, four times. I saw it three times and never got tired of it and that's a very unusual thing for me, particularly with something that's based on my work because I know the story inside and out. You see the movie once and you say, 'well, okay, I can move on with my life.' There are a couple of movies where I go back and, you know, the experience is enriched by the previous viewing. So, is the Shawshank Redemption, there's one. *Cujo* is another one. I see new things in those movies all the

SS. Georgie movie prop,
IT Chapter Two, 2019

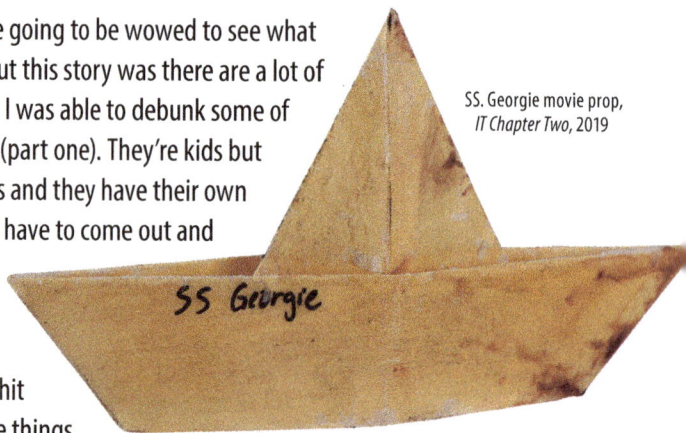

SS Georgie

OCTOBER

22 THURSDAY　　　**23** FRIDAY　　　**24** SATURDAY

25 SUNDAY

time. But, the re-experiencing of *IT*, I can understand why people, particularly young people went to see it again and again and again because they're the people 18, 19-year-olds who are the most in-touch with the children that they were at that age. And, they make an emotional connection with the kids and that's a great thing. One of the things that Andy understands, as a filmmaker, is that you have to care about the people in the story. With *IT*, Andy put the people first. He put the kids first and in the second movie, the interaction between the adults and the children show up in flashbacks and sometimes parts of the story that are more illuminated from the first part. There are, he revisits moments from the first movie but we see a wider perspective because we see an adult perspective there. So, Andy puts the people first, and, as a result, you have an old-fashioned movie experience where you root for the good guys."

Larry Fire with *IT* director Andy Muschietti at a press screening of *IT*. August 2017

OCTOBER

26 MONDAY

27 TUESDAY

28 WEDNESDAY

IT CHAPTER TWO: PENNYWISE MAKE-UP DISPLAY

This one-of-a-kind item of Pennywise the Dancing Clown went up for auction. Based on Bill Skarsgård's torso this make-up display is from the production of Andy Muschietti's horror sequel *IT Chapter Two*. Originating from a prosthetics make-up artist on the production, this display features a bust modelled on Skarsgård, upon which production-made and painted facial appliances, enlarged cranium cowl, and acrylic teeth inserts have been added. The display is finished with hand-punched, replica faux ginger hair, hand-painted glass eyes and a replica Pennywise torso and intentionally distressed clown attire. The production-made elements of the display have been carefully repaired and restored. Dimensions (display): 38 cm x 74 cm x 67 cm (15" x 29 1/4" x 26 1/2"). Estimated to sell for: £6,000 - £12,000. The Winning bid: £40,950 ($55,000 US). It had 25 bids.

OCTOBER

29 THURSDAY

30 FRIDAY

31 SATURDAY
Halloween

1 SUNDAY
Daylight Saving Time End

Pennywise makeup display, **propstore.com**

NOVEMBER

2 MONDAY
Day of the Dead

3 TUESDAY

4 WEDNESDAY

STEPHEN KING'S CAMEO DAY FOR *LARGO*

I know, you're asking "what Largo film?" Good question. While filming *IT Chapter Two* they used a fake name so it hopefully wouldn't be noticed that *IT Chapter Two* was being filmed in Port Hope, Ontario. It was used on the actor's chairs, scripts, in advance interviews so they could keep the filming under wraps. Of course, some Stephen King and film fans figured it out early on since the crew had come back to Port Hope, using the name "Derry" in storefronts, the police station, etc. all around the town. Not to mention there was one Pennywise the clown sitting on top of the Paul Bunyon statue in town for a while. Wait, where did that statue come from? That's right they had Paul Bunyon statue made just for the film (I wonder if it was allowed to stay?). As the local online paper NorthumberlandNews.com reported "Port Hope Mayor

King and Sanderson. Photo Bob Sanderson 2017

Bob Sanderson, welcomed Stephen King to Port Hope on Sept. 11. King visited the community for the filming of 'Largo,' the sequel to *IT*, which continues *IT*, in full swing, Port Hope Mayor Bob Sanderson said the cast and crew have become part of the community. . ." Sanderson got to

NOVEMBER

5 THURSDAY

6 FRIDAY

7 SATURDAY

8 SUNDAY

meet the American author on the set while filming at a downtown business on Sept. 11th. "It was lovely, he is a lovely man," he said of the encounter, adding that King is very down to earth and casual. "Stephen King himself absolutely loves the community. I don't think everybody recognizes him so he did go out and it was an incognito sort of thing." Sanderson said they shared a laugh when King pointed to the button for re-election he was wearing and said, "If I lived here I would vote for you." Sanderson said he feels it's his obligation to welcome everyone to the community, whether it's new ministers forming the government or the author of horror, supernatural fiction, suspense, science fiction and fantasy himself. "Mr. King himself, the director and the crew are just great," the mayor added. "They have become part of the community." "This filming will go on and the community has really engaged with it and are enjoying it," he said. Asked about King's impressions of Port Hope, Sanderson said he likes small towns so he felt very comfortable and welcome here. "He did meet some of the people here because he wanted to, and he was very gracious in making his time available," he said, pointing out that the author was very busy while on the set, putting in 12 hours on the day he saw him. "He is very generous in his comments and I gave him an election button even though he can't vote for me."

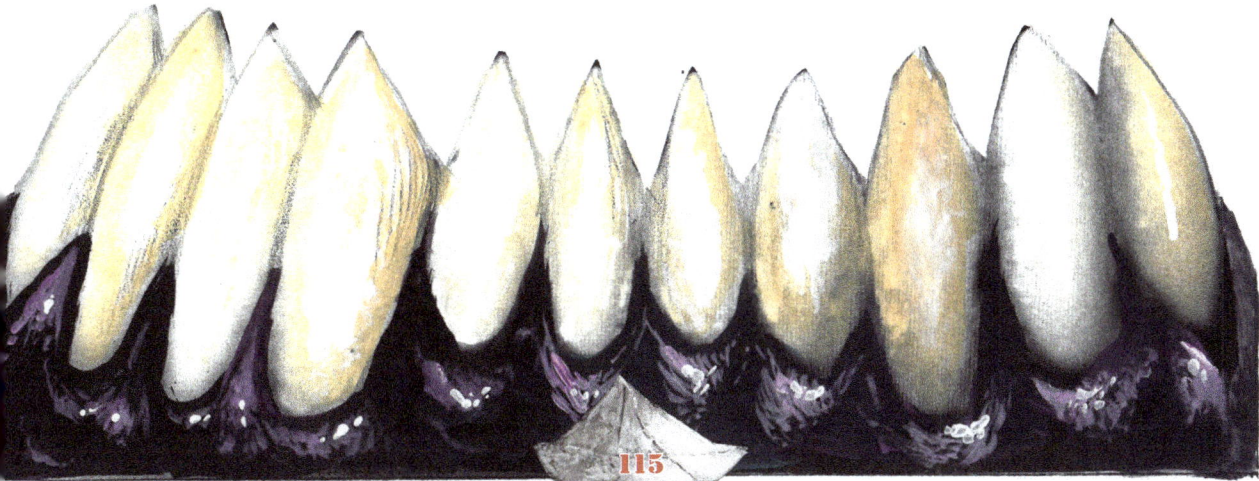

DERRY'S CANAL DAYS FESTIVAL

9 MONDAY

10 TUESDAY

11 WEDNESDAY
Veterans Day

IT'S BEEN A LONG TIME COMING

On September 12, 2025, Stephen King's *The Long Walk* opened in theaters. It's been a long time coming. After years, decades, of attempts to bring *The Long Walk* to the big screen it was announced in 2024 that this devastating novel from Stephen King (as Richard Bachman) was to begin filming that year. They filmed it in Manitoba, Winnipeg, and surrounding areas in Canada. This was exciting news finally for King fans as it was repeatedly considered for the big screen by many famous directors. George Romero gave it a try in the late '80s; Frank Darabont, who had the option for years (*The Shawshank Redemption*, *The Mist*), began

The Long Walk, Scribner 2025

NOVEMBER

12 THURSDAY

13 FRIDAY

14 SATURDAY

15 SUNDAY

developing a version in the late 2000s. In 2019, *Scary Stories to Tell in the Dark* filmmaker André Øvredal was attached to direct. Each stumbling at their attempts. It takes a lot to make a film, from belief to finance, and a lot of issues can get in the way.

To celebrate the films release Scribner released a movie-cover trade paperback and for the first time in trade hardcover (there was a short run limited release in 2023) since the original

The Long Walk, New King Cover Series by Glenn Chadbourne.
Order at **StephenKingCatalog.com**

paperbacks release on July 3rd, 1979. The first print run for *The Long Walk* hardcover only had 11,000 copies published. At the time of this writing, it was going into a second printing. You can find First Printing hardcovers at **StephenKingCatalog.com**

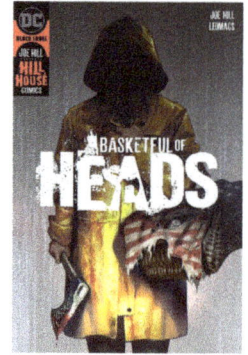

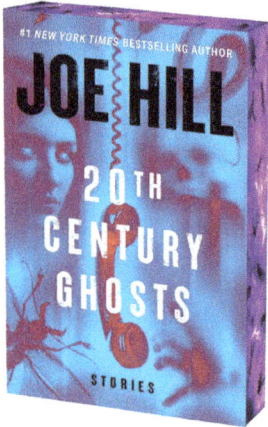

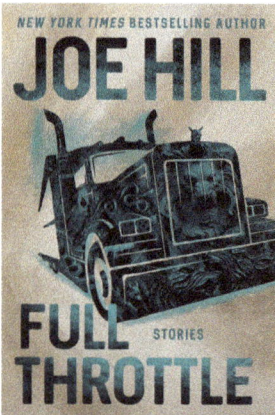

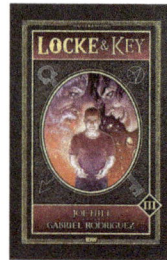

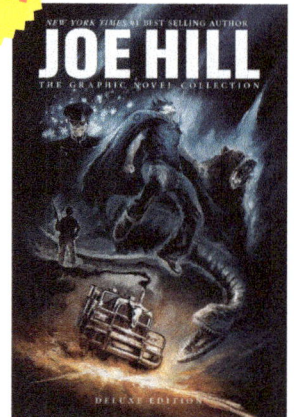

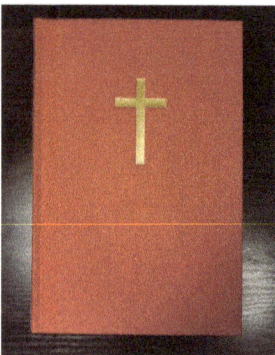

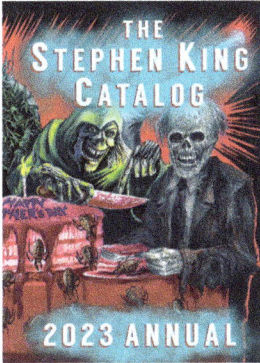

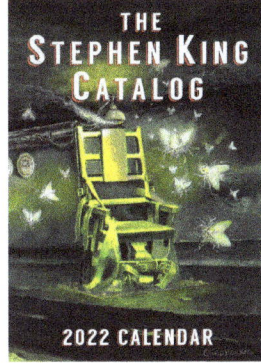

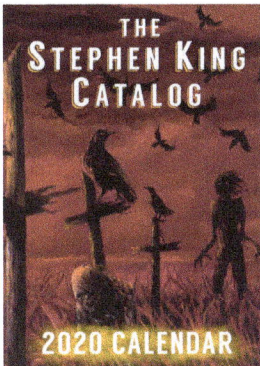

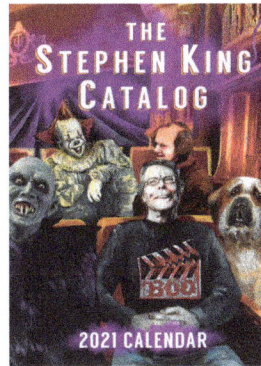

NOVEMBER

16 MONDAY

17 TUESDAY

18 WEDNESDAY

THE KIDS ARE ALRIGHT

"I was at first a bit intimidated by my all-star cast, but my fears were unfounded — they all turned out to be generous and supportive team players. The child actors were much more of a challenge ... I'm especially proud of the adult/child pairings, as I think we made really astute choices and got really lucky making it believable that that group of seven kids grew up to be that group of seven adults, which is no easy feat."

—Tommy Lee Wallace, 2015, director of *IT* 1990 ABC series.

NOVEMBER

19 THURSDAY   **20** FRIDAY   **21** SATURDAY

22 SUNDAY

IT series press photo, ABC 1990

Adam Faraizi, Emily Perkins, Jonathan Brandis, Marlon Alfonzo Taylor, Seth Green and Ben Heller (l-r, top photo), portray friends who meet in the woods to seek out and destroy an evil entity that has already killed one child and continues to haunt the rest of them. Three decades later, Dennis Christopher, Annette O'Toole, Richard Thomas, John Ritter and Harry Anderson (l-r, bottom), as the same loyal group of friends, reunite to destroy the evil entity that has returned to their hometown after 30 years to kill again, on the ABC Novel for Television, **STEPHEN KING'S "IT,"** airing **SUNDAY, NOV. 18** and **TUESDAY, NOV. 20** (9:00-11:00 p.m., ET, both days), on the ABC Television Network.   Photo credit: Chris Helcermonas Benge/ABC.
JP 10/30/90   27543A-1

23 MONDAY   **24** TUESDAY   **25** WEDNESDAY

WHAT'S IN YOUR WALLET?

IT Canadian Full-Length VHS Screening Copy 1992 - VGA 85 NM+, Flatback Seal / Rear WB Logo Watermarks, Warner Home Video. 1990's small-screen adaptation of Stephen King's bestseller features an all-star cast featuring an iconic turn by Tim Curry as the evil Pennywise. King's story centers on seven children who must fight an intergalactic demon posing as a child-killing clown. Years later they reunite after the killings begin again and they realize that they didn't complete the job the first time.

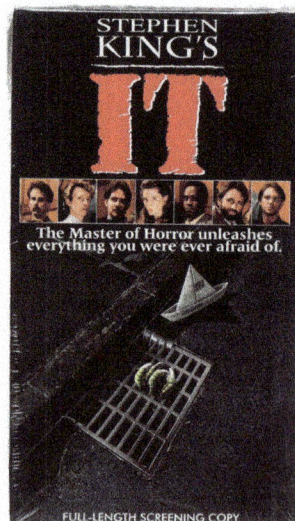

IT Screener photo by **ha.com**

NOVEMBER

26 THURSDAY
Thanksgiving

27 FRIDAY

28 SATURDAY

29 SUNDAY

IT Screener
photo by **ha.com**

This full-length Canadian VHS screening copy features an alternate cover to the regular retail cover that closely resembles the novels' original cover and has received an overall grade of 85 NM+ by VGA with matching Box and Seal subgrades of 85. This sealed set sold on Oct 31 (Halloween!), 2022 for: $2,500.00. The buyer has it relisted for bids of $3,750 or more. What's in your wallet? Available at **HA.com**

30 MONDAY

1 TUESDAY

2 WEDNESDAY

THE RUNNING MAN, FINALLY CROSSES THE FINISH LINE

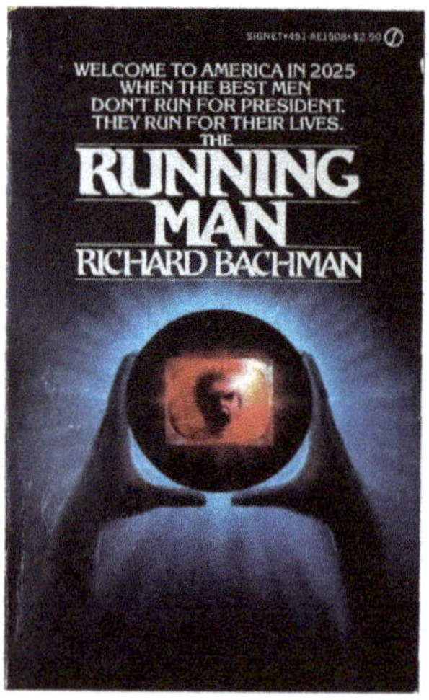

The first paperback release of *The Running Man* was in May 1982, published by Signet as a paperback original. It was written under Stephen King's pseudonym Richard Bachman and was the fourth novel published under that name. This is the first edition release of *The Running Man*.

Now, 43 years later, *The Running Man* finally received its first-ever hardcover release from Scribner, October 14th, 2025. There were only 7,500 copies printed of this first printing, making it one of the smallest print runs of a Stephen King hardcover. As of this writing it has going into a second printing.

First printings can still be purchase at **StephenKingCatalog.com**

The Running Man, 1st Printing Paperback. Signet, May 1982

DECEMBER

3 THURSDAY

4 FRIDAY

5 SATURDAY

6 SUNDAY

The Running Man, 1st Printing, Hardocver, Scribners 2025

First printing hardcover available at

StephenKingCatalog.com

Dust jacket comes wrapped in an archival book cover

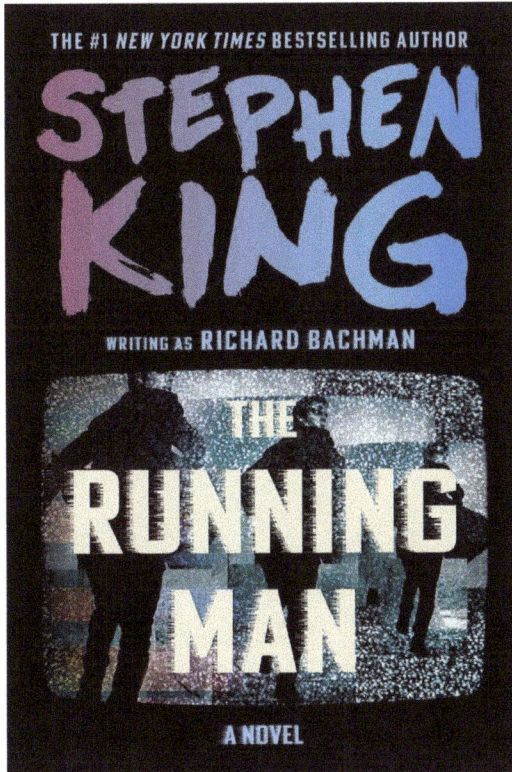

7 MONDAY

8 TUESDAY

9 WEDNESDAY

WHO... IS ROBIN FURTH?

When Stephen King readers opened up their copy of *Never Flinch* (May 27th, 2025) they discovered the book was dedicated to... ***For Robin Furth, with love and thanks for all your hard work***
– Stephen King

Robin Furth began her association with Stephen King when her college professor, King's previous professor, Burt Hatlen, asked her if she would like to help Stephen King with research for the next three "Dark Tower" novels. She gladly accepted. After researching all the previous "Dark Tower" novels for him, to bring him up-to-speed on who, what, where, when in those novels she became quite the expert of Mid-world, All-World, and everything within that realm. To the point that she became a co-creator with some of "The Dark Tower" graphic series with all her knowledge in that world. Go take a look at your collection, her name is on all of those releases.

Never Flinch New Stephen King Cover series.
Art by Glenn Chadbourne 2025

DECEMBER

10 THURSDAY

11 FRIDAY

12 SATURDAY
Hanukkah (1st day)

13 SUNDAY

Robin was then recruited to help with research with the Bill Hodges trilogy which continued with the Holly character stories (I believe seven appearances) and this obviously led to the last (?) book with Holly in *Never Flinch*. After decades of working with Stephen King on, and with, his fiction she deserves this recognition.

We took it a step further and with our New Stephen King Cover series we create with artist Glenn Chadbourne, we added her likeness to the *Never Flinch* cover with Steve's dedication. You can see the cover and her image on the back flap. Robin Furth's dedication to Stephen King's work these decades deserves this second honor, the first being from the man himself. *Thank you, Robin, for all you do in the world of King, for all of us.* — Dave Hinchberger

You can order this cover, and see the New Stephen King Cover series at **StephenKingCatalog.com**

14 MONDAY

15 TUESDAY

16 WEDNESDAY

IT CHAPTER TWO – SS Georgie Paper Boat

'It's still down here, everything floats down here, we'll float, Bill, we'll all float — '
– IT as Georgie

An SS Georgie paper boat from Andy Muschietti's horror sequel *IT Chapter Two*. Bill's (James McAvoy) younger brother George (Jackson Robert Scott) perished at the hands of It while playing with his paper boat, the SS Georgie. The boat is made of paper, covered with wax to make it waterproof. It is stained with faux blood and "SS Georgie" is handwritten in black marker on one side. The wax has cracked and come away in some places. Dimensions: 25.5 cm x 13.5 cm (10" x 5 1/4"). This prop from the film was auctioned off with the estimate being: £800 - £1,200. The winning bid came at the end of 32 total bids and exceeded the auctions expectations selling at £18,900 / $25,215 US dollars.

SS. Georgie movie prop, *IT Chapter Two*, 2019

DECEMBER

17 THURSDAY

18 FRIDAY

19 SATURDAY

20 SUNDAY

YOU'LL

FLOAT

TOO.

IT

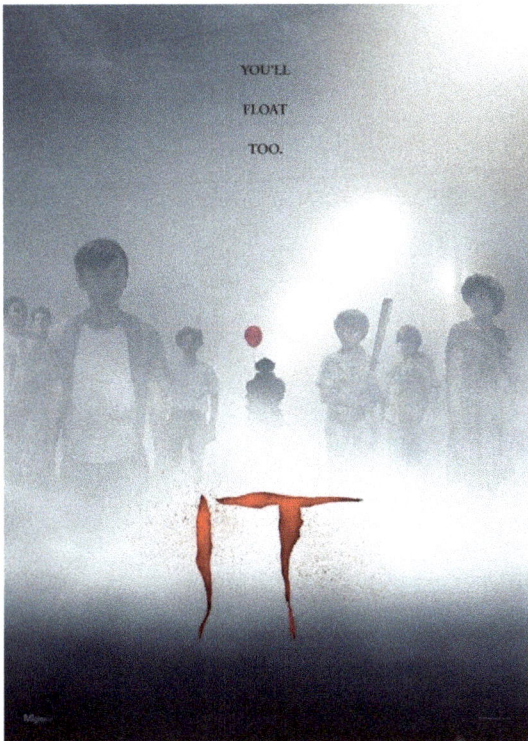

IT poster available at **filmcellsltd.com**

TURTLE ENVY

One of the most inevitable cuts from the source material for *IT CHAPTER TWO* was the choice to leave out Maturin, The Turtle who is an important part of the novel but offered some logistical issues on account of being both giant and a turtle. In the book, Maturin created the universe (specially, it vomited it up after a stomach ache) and helps guide Bill through the Ritual of Chüd to find how to defeat It the first time. He's absent from the films, but just as there was a nod to him in the first film, a turtle statue

Hero Ritual of Chud Artifact, *IT Chapter Two*. Sold at auction for £11,250 / 15,014 US dollars

DECEMBER

24 THURSDAY
Christmas Eve

25 FRIDAY
Christmas Day

26 SATURDAY
Kwanzaa

27 SUNDAY

appears in the second as a nod to him. And not only that, when the turtle appears on the desk in a classroom, the camera makes sure to frame it so there's a globe behind it, so it appears on his back. That's a nice little reference to the fact that Maturin carries the universe on the back of his shell. It's not the only reference to the giant turtle either. In the final sequence, when the Losers' are fighting back against Pennywise, he lashes out verbally with what is clearly the worst insult he can think of calling them "filthy Maturin." Out of context, it makes no sense, but it's a great little insight into Its deep-rooted hatred of its old enemy.

Hero Ritual of Chud Artifact top. Notice The Turtle image

DECEMBER

28 MONDAY

29 TUESDAY

30 WEDNESDAY
New Year's Eve

DYING FROM LAUGHTER

A Richard Tozier (Bill Hader) funeral service card from Andy Muschietti's horror sequel *IT Chapter Two*. Richie is taunted by Pennywise and given a card for his own funeral service. The front features a picture of Richie and details of the service, and the back features a disparaging summation of Richie's life, written by Pennywise. Notice the cemetery name at the bottom of the card? Mount Hope Cemetery, from *Pet Sematary*. Dimensions: 21.5 cm x 14 cm (8.5" x 5.5") This card was auctioned off and had an estimate of £300 - £600. The fourth bid won at £756 / $1008 US dollars.

IN LOVING MEMORY
of

RICHARD TOZIER
1976 - 2016

FUNERAL SERVICE
TO BE HELD AT:
FIRST METHODIST CHURCH OF DERRY
REVEREND RAYMOND FOGARTY - OFFICIATING

INTERMENT:
MOUNT HOPE CEMETERY

JANUARY

3̶1̶ THURSDAY
New Year's Day

1̶ FRIDAY

2 SATURDAY

3 SUNDAY

THE DAILY DERRY

A copy of *The Daily Derry* newspaper from Andy Muschietti's horror sequel *IT Chapter Two*. *The Daily Derry* can be seen in newspaper dispensers in the film as the Losers' make their way across the town. It features the headline "Body Parts Found In Barrens" and a filler article about a crime in Malaysia. The article underneath (credited to assistant art director David Best) features a synopsis and history of Stanley Kubrick's *The Shining*. Dimensions (open): 55 cm x 32.5 cm (21 3/4" x 12 3/4"). This item was auctioned with an estimate: £600 - £800. It sold on the 5th bid at £1,134 / $1,512 US dollars

The Daily Derry

BODY PARTS FOUND IN BARRENS
Authorities probe link to Dennis Torrio and Dawn Roy cases

CRIME SCENE DO NOT CRO

Fremlin 'non-apology' plunges Lib Dems into fresh chaos

2026 Stephen King Calendar: IT Pennywise Has Arrived
© 2025 by Overlook Connection Press.

"Pennywise Turns Forty" and all text, unless otherwise noted, within the calendar section,
© 2025 by Dave Hinchberger.
"Pennywise in the Flesh: Interview Excerpt with Tim Curry", ©1990, 2025 by Steve Newton.
"Stephen King's *IT* – The Miniseries," © 2025 by L.L. Soares.
"Welcome to My Town, Derry," © 2025 by Chris Jiggins.
Excerpts from *IT*, © 1986 by Stephen King, Pages 22, 23,
"Inspiration For *IT*" © by Stephen King, StephenKing.com
Unless otherwise noted, cover and all artwork within
© 2025 by Glenn Chadbourne

Layout, design, and border re-creations (of Glenn Chadbourne art)
by Bryan McAllister, Fine Dog Creative.

Published © 2025 by Overlook Connection Press.
PO Box 1934, Hiram, Georgia 30141
Visit us at:
StephenKingCatalog.com OverlookConnection.com

First Printing ISBN: 9781623307110

VISIT OUR SOCIAL MEDIA to keep up with items posted daily.

🧵 stephenkingcatalog   f stephenkingcatalog   𝕏 @StephenKingCat
📷 stephenkingcatalog   🦋 @stephenkingcatalog.bsky.social

Page 2: *IT* book covers from around the world

ROW

Row	Covers
1st	Ukrane – Bulgaria – United States – Greece – US Limited
2nd	United States – Lithuania – Poland – Hebrew – Russia
3rd	Sweden – Russia – Italy – United States – Unknown
4th	Spain – United States – United States – United States – Netherlands
5th	Russia – Japan – United States – United Kingdom – France

BIBLIOGRAPHY, END NOTES, IMAGES

PAGE: 1 King, Stephen. *IT*, Hodder & Stoughton 1986

PAGE: 5 Pennywise Turns Forty! © 2025 Dave Hinchberger

PAGES: 6-8 Tim Curry interview photos, cover, *Fangoria* No. 99, © 1990 *Fangoria*

PAGE: 6 Steven Newton photo © 2025 by Dawn Newton

PAGE: 7 *IT* miniseries logo, © 1990 ABC TV

PAGES: 14-18 Photos © 2025 by Chris Jiggins

PAGE: 26 Pennywise and the kids cast press photo, ABC TV 1990

PAGE: 27 *MAD* Magazine, No. 297, September 1990

PAGE: 28 Stephen King, *IT* novel, Viking 1986

PAGE: 32 *IT* poster. Signed by artist Timothy Pittides. Only 65 copies screenprinted

PAGE: 34 Pennywise 7" AF figure, Diamond Select

PAGE: 39 Shinola Ox-Blood shoe polish wax tin. 1940's

PAGE: 44 1962 Schwinn Jaguar Mark IV

PAGE: 46 Stephen King, *Life of Chuck* X Post, June 2025

PAGE: 47 Karen Gillan, *Life of Chuck* X Post, June 2025

PAGES: 56-57 *Jeopardy*, April 25th 2025, © NBC TV

PAGES: 58-61 "Inspiration For IT" © by Stephen King

PAGES: 64-65 Cameron Thomson, Vancouverisawesome.com, 10-21-2021

PAGES: 74-77 "Romero's IT", an excerpt with Lawrence D. Cohen. *Pennywise: The Story of IT*, © 2021 Cinedigm

PAGES: 78-79 Charlie Howard, by Stephen King Bangordailynews.com © 2014

PAGES: 75 Group photo © 2025 Lawrence D. Cohen

PAGE: 80 Pennywise t-shirt image, © 2025 Pennywise band

PAGE: 81 *Pennywise* album cover, © 1991 Pennywise band

PAGES: 84-85 Mark Hamill on *Jimmy Kimmel Live*, © 2025 ABC TV

PAGES: 86-87 Tommy Lee Wallace interview, © 2025 Anthony Northrup

PAGES: 92-95 The Look of IT, Interview excerpt with Bart Mixon © 2025 Andrew Rausch

PAGE: 97 *IT Chapter Two* cast signed poster, propstore.com

PAGES: 108-109 King in Port Hope, NorthumberlandNews.com © 2018

PAGES: 110 & 128 S.S. Georgie boat movie prop. Propstore.com

PAGE: 120 Tommy Lee Wallace quote, *Pennywise: The Story of IT* © 2021 Cinedigm

PAGES: 130-131 Hero Ritual of Chud Artifact prop. Propstore. com

PAGES: 132 Richie Tozier funeral card prop, *IT Chapter Two*. Propstore.com

PAGE: 133 *Daily Derry* newspaper, *IT Chapter Two*. Propstore. com

Glenn Chadbourne art: Cover and all calendar border art Copyright © 2025. Pages 20, 22, 24, 38, 45, 58, 60, 64, 117, 126, 127

Allen Koszowski art: Pages 23, 59, 62, 76

2025 Stephen King Annual On Tour Limited Edition

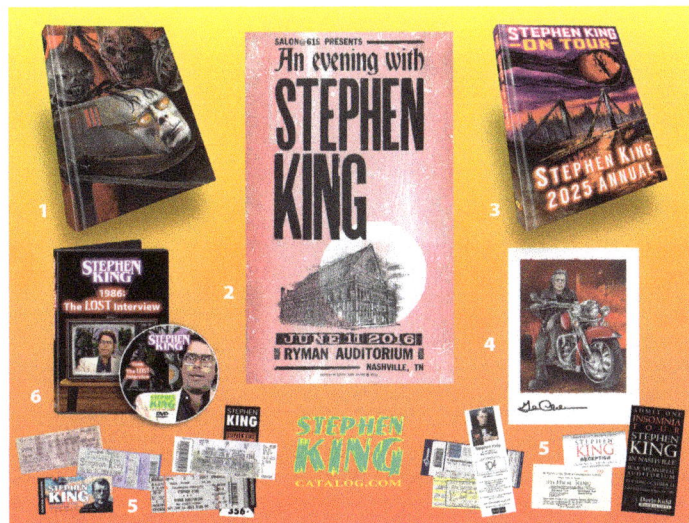

Only 500 Sets!

1. **Stephen King Limited "Train" Cover, Signed/ Numbered by artist Glenn Chadbourne**

2. **Stephen King frameable An Evening with Stephen King tour poster**

3. ***2025 Stephen King Annual.* Signed / Numbered by Dave Hinchberger**

4. **Stephen King as "Bachman," Signed Art card by Glenn Chadbourne**

5. **Stephen King Commemorative Tickets, pack of 12.**

6. **A DVD of a Lost Stephen King Interview from his *Tommyknockers* Tour in 1986.**

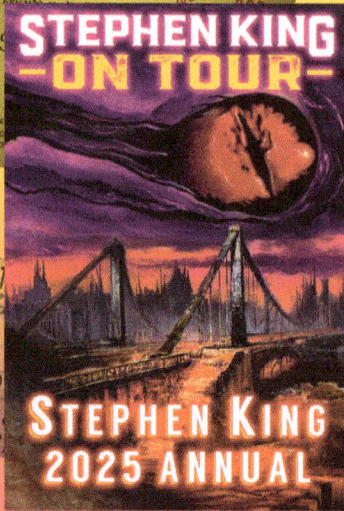

2025 STEPHEN KING ANNUAL: ON TOUR!

The 2025 Stephen King Annual! Articles, interviews, book/movie reviews and a 52-week Calendar of Facts and Trivia in Full-Color!

This year's theme celebrating Stephen King on Tour!

Stephen King has had many book store signings, tour readings at colleges, libraries, auditoriums (like at the Ryman, the Grand Ole' Opry in Nashville!) including church and drive-in theaters! Here we delve into these appearances and we hear from fans and readers who share their personal experiences from the last forty years.

▶ **Dave Hinchberger's** Introduction: **Stephen King, Rock n' Roll Hoochie Koo!** Plus, insights into Stephen King's tours over the years.

▶ Award-winning artist **Glenn Chadbourne's** original wrap-around cover exclusively created for the 2025 Annual as well as original artwork featured throughout this 250 plus page full-color hardcover.

▶ **Bev Vincent's "The first time I met Stephen King"** Stephen King instore with King's mentor and author, Don Robertson, over thirty-five years ago. Mr. Vincent's annual write-up of **Everything King – Current and Upcoming.**

▶ **Kevin Quigley - "Do the Collapse"** - Kevin recounts his Stephen King in person appearance. **Tour Schedules** - Kevin also lays out his research of Stephen King tours over forty years of appearances!

▶ **Stephen Spignesi - The New Lost Work of Stephen King** annual in-depth look at the current and rare appearances of original Stephen King short fiction.

▶ **Andrew Rausch** interviews Ridley Pearson. Touring with Stephen King in their band, **The Rock Bottom Remainders!**

▶ **L.L. Soares** takes a deeper look into the films and TV of director / screenwriter, Mike Flanigan, who is currently working to bring *The Dark Tower* to the screen.

▶ **Noah Mitchel & Diana Petroff** Stephen King collectibles titled **"Extreme King."** They will examine in-depth the releases of *Firestarter*, including the Asbestos Lettered edition. A unique release in the Stephen King canon of limited editions.

▶ **Hank Wagner** Looks at *Sleeping Beauties*, novel and graphic adaptation.

▶ **Anthony Northrup** annual Dollar Baby Review featuring Julia Marchese's wonderful creation of the short, **"I Know What You Need"**, film with a review and interview.

▶ **Dave Hinchberger's** annual calendar features fifty-two weeks of trivia and facts around each Annual's theme. It's time to go *On Tour* with Stephen King with quotes, facts, informative articles, covering the years of visits with Stephen King and the many guests along the way he encounters. You'll enjoy the information and illustrations within these Annuals for years to come. There is so much more within! Too much to list here! Visit StephenKingCatalog.com for complete details. | Signed by Dave Hinchberger! |

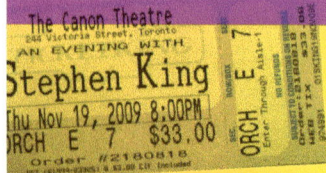

Published by Overlook Connection Press
PO Box 1934 Hiram, GA 30141

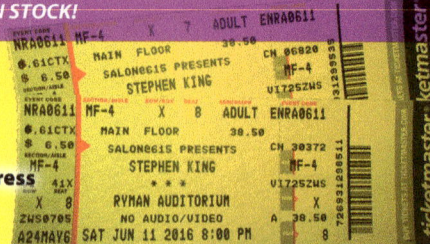